CORE FOCUSED
FAMILY THERAPY

CORE FOCUSED FAMILY THERAPY

MOVING FROM CHAOS TO CLARITY

Judye Hess, PhD, and Ross Cohen, MA

Idyll Arbor

Published and Distributed by

Idyll Arbor, Inc.

PO Box 720, Ravensdale, WA 98051 (360) 825-7797

To the best of our knowledge, the information and recommendations of this book reflect currently accepted practice. Nevertheless, they cannot be considered absolute and universal. Recommendations must be considered in light of needs and condition. The authors and publisher disclaim responsibly for any adverse effects resulting directly or indirectly from the suggested management practices, from any undetected errors, or from the reader's misunderstanding of the text.

Library of Congress Cataloging-in-Publication Data
Hess, Judye, 1944-
  Core focused family therapy : moving from chaos to clarity / Judye Hess and Ross Cohen.
    p. ; cm.
  Includes bibliographical references and index.
  ISBN 978-1-882883-70-7 (alk. paper)
  1. Family psychotherapy. I. Cohen, Ross, 1970- II. Title.
  [DNLM: 1. Family Therapy--methods. WM 430.5.F2 H586c 2008]
  RC488.5.H47 2008
  616.89'156--dc22
                                                            2008013623

ISBN 9781882883707

To my students and their families who were willing to take the risk of opening their hearts and minds to trust me and the process of family therapy.
And to my own family, past and present, who have supported me in the development of my career as a family therapist.

Contents

ACKNOWLEDGMENTS

To Ross Cohen, LPC, my former student and co-author, who believed that, in addition to my teaching the traditional masters of family therapy such as Whitaker, Satir, and Minuchin, I had "an incredible system of my own that I modeled every week, but did not teach per se." After taking all my classes, Ross signed up for an independent study with me while studying in the Integral Counseling Psychology program at the California Institute of Integral Studies, and asked me questions about my style of family therapy, what I was thinking, and why I did what I did. By studying my responses, he discovered certain themes and principles, which he compiled and then compared with transcripts of sessions I had done in class with actual families. Ross wrote a paper on my style of therapy entitled, "Capturing the Magic: The Principles and Techniques of Judye Hess' Family Therapy" which became the core of the text I have expanded into this book.

To Mary Coombs, PhD, LCSW, my friend and colleague who teaches family therapy at University of California in Berkeley and University of San Francisco. Over the last several years, Mary has invited me to demonstrate my family work with students in her classes. When I gave her a short form of this book to distribute to her students before my visit, she encouraged me to consider getting it published, something I hadn't even contemplated before that. Also, to my sister, Marlene Gershman Paley, PhD, a psychoanalyst in NY, who read the original manuscript and provided her unending support for my continuing this project. To Tom Blaschko, my editor and publisher from Idyll Arbor Inc., who enthusiastically agreed to take the project on and work with me to expand it to the book it now is.

To my dear friend Mel Hecker, a professional development editor, who worked with me on editing the book from its earliest forms. To my colleague and mentor, Michael Kahn, PhD, a fellow teacher at California Institute of Integral Studies, who read the book early on and made some important contributions. To Peter Geiger, former student and present friend and colleague, whose skill with language was a tremendous contribution in helping me to refine some of the text in this book.

To Alan Leveton, MD, one of my first and most important teachers of family therapy, who was an early reader of the book, made some important suggestions, and encouraged me to have it published by expressing his belief that the book would make an important contribution to the family therapy field. Alan, along with other dear Bay Area colleagues: Dan Wile, PhD, Martin Kirschenbaum, PhD, Rodney Shapiro, PhD, Terrence Patterson, PhD, and Brad Keeney, PhD, gave me tremendous support and encouragement with their glowing reviews of the book, for which I am extremely grateful.

To the California Institute of Integral Studies and the Integral Counseling Psychology program in particular, for giving me the opportunity to teach this alternative, experiential family therapy class for the last 25 years. Being part of this wonderful community has allowed me to come in contact with the exceptional student body, without whom this book would never have been written.

Of course, without my parents, Ada and Harry Gershman,

providing the raw material for my devotion to this field, the book would never have been written. I especially want to thank my father, Harry Gershman, psychiatrist, psychoanalyst, and Dean of the Karen Horney Institute in New York City for many years. He introduced me to the field of psychology at a very young age, and inspired both my sister and me to become psychotherapists ourselves. I am most thankful to my parents for their enduring support and encouragement of my education and I know that, if they were alive today, they would be very proud of me.

And finally, to my loving partner, Simon Friedman, whose unending emotional and technical support, have helped me stay focused on the writing of this book. Simon, along with our two kitties, Ripple and Sabrina, has provided a profound sense of nourishment and ease in my life for which I am extremely grateful.

— Judye Hess

To Judye Hess, who inspired me as both a teacher and clinician, and who took the time to work with me so that I could deepen my understanding of family therapy. The work that I did with Judye, which is integrated into this text, has been invaluable to me as a clinician in all realms of therapy, far beyond family therapy alone. Also, to those who helped me find my way as a therapist: John Prendergast, Adyashanti, Lucanna Grey, Derek Pehle, Philip Brooks, and Alan Kubler. To my clients, past and present, who have taught me so much. Finally, special thanks to Randa, my loving wife, who has always supported and believed in me.

— Ross Cohen

Preface

Two brothers, both of whom had become journalists in their adult lives, wound up on opposite sides of the political spectrum. Having had some major disagreements, they hadn't spoken in four years. When interviewed by a third journalist after their four-year hiatus, the "dialogue" was not exactly warm and fuzzy and it occurred in public. Toward the end of this epic get-together, the interviewer asked them if they were friends.

One brother answered, "No. There was an old joke in East Germany that went, 'Are the Russians our friends or our brothers?' And the answer is, 'They must be our brothers because we can choose our friends.'"

The other brother replied, "The great thing about family life is that it introduces you to people you would otherwise never meet."

And this is the dilemma we face in being part of a family. Although these people are among the most important relationships in our lives, and influence so much of who we become as adults, we never really got to choose them. We are thrown into our lives in such a mysterious way that we will probably never understand why we were born here and not there, now and not then.

The problems we face as family therapists are germane to this issue. Families often have members with different values, ideals, and temperaments. Because they are family, they often remain together to perform tasks and to exchange love and affection even though the other people in the family are people with whom they "might never have chosen to connect." Expectations run rampant for parents as well as for children. At one extreme we have children imagining they were mixed up at the hospital and have come home with the wrong parents. Some parents wring their hands and exclaim, "No child of mine could ever be like this!" The situation becomes even more complicated when parents have children who, in their opinion, are the wrong gender, the wrong sexual orientation, or have physical or psychological disabilities for which the parents did not plan. The reactions to these events run the gamut from murder and suicide to parents doing everything they possibly can for the child because, after all, he is their own flesh and blood.

Despite the 1950s images of the "Cleaver" family or "Father Knows Best," many families do not have a healthy, cooperative, loving, or joyous connection. For families who suffer any form of dysfunctionality, family therapy is a tool that can be incredibly helpful if not transformative in their relationships. Even for families that already have close relationships but want to work toward a deeper level of interacting with one another, family therapy can facilitate this growth.

In the following pages you will see the myriad ways in which family treatment can enhance the lives of the family members who participate in this endeavor. Core Focused Family Therapy is one way that the practitioner can help clients achieve more fulfillment in these crucial relationships and get to experience these "people we would otherwise never meet" in a far more honest and loving way.

Introduction

This book is intended for graduate students in psychology; professionals in the field who are thinking of including family therapy in their practice; child and adolescent therapists who are interested in working with the whole family; teachers, trainers, and supervisors of students of family therapy who are looking for a way to educate their students in an experiential model.

The book is divided into three sections:

Section I covers the general principles and values of Core Focused Family Therapy (CFFT), desirable qualities of a therapist who may choose to include this practice in his methodology, as well as how it fits into the mainstream of other schools of family therapy. Included will be a summary of the background and some of the basic tenets of the family therapy movement, including an understanding of the paradigm shift from individual to systems thinking.

Section II provides a detailed description of how to put CFFT into use in a very practical, hands-on way. This part of the book will include the "pre-initial session," the "check-in," the "direct interaction," the "check-out," subsequent sessions, termination, and, finally, a section on common mistakes made by CFFT family therapists.

Section III provides descriptions of two alternative methods of using CFFT when the whole family or parts of the family cannot be present: Psychodramatic Family Therapy and Gestalt empty chair techniques. These methodologies are especially useful for educators of family therapists and facilitators of Psychodramatic Family Therapy work, but can also be used directly in actual family therapy sessions, or individually with one or more clients.

Section I

Overview of CFFT

1.
General Principles and Values of CFFT

In **Core Focused Family Therapy (CFFT)** a context is created wherein family members' **core interpersonal truths** can be discovered and communicated to other members of their family. This method attempts to combine **individual, interpersonal,** and **systemic** growth and healing in family sessions.

The CFFT therapist begins to work with **individual** family members in the context of the family setting to help each of them to reach clarity about their own **core** feelings and thoughts, and subsequently to express these **interpersonal truths** to other family members. As one family member gets in touch with his frustrated desires, deep resentments, jealousies, and disappointments, as well as with his love and longing for connection with another member, he is helped by the therapist to communicate these feelings directly to that person from a place of openness and authenticity. Upon hearing this, the receiving person is typically inspired by the honesty and vulnerability in the communication, and is then helped by the therapist to respond in a similar fashion. This kind of **direct interaction** between the two family members results in a change in the **interpersonal** connection between them, as they become more empathic about one another's joy, pain, and perspective. The authenticity that is fostered by this process allows for the development of safety and mutual understanding among family members that is crucial in rebuilding the trust that has often been sacrificed over years of pain and misunderstanding.

Any change in the relationship between two family members will affect the other members of the group who have been observing the interactions in an emotionally engaged manner. Subsequently, the other members become inspired to take their own risks in **directly interacting** with family members about their own **core issues** until the whole system has taken on a new dynamic, thus inducing **systemic** change.

When a person is in contact with his core truths about who he is and what he wants and needs, he is in a much better position to make healthy decisions about the kinds of relationships he wants to have with other people in his life, including his family members. So often, one's psyche is burdened by the early childhood roles taken on to allow oneself and one's family to survive. Many children become the caretakers of parents that need their help and sacrifice their own needs in the process. Years later, they find themselves continuing this caretaker role in their own intimate relationships and even seeking out mates who need care-taking. Furthermore, as adults, they are still fearful of "rocking the boat" with a family member whom they and other members have labeled as "fragile" or "explosive." They fear that if they were to confront such an individual, that person might "fall apart" and they would wind up with a much worse relationship and be burdened by feelings of guilt. So they continue to suppress their feelings in that person's presence, as well as in similar situations outside the family circle and, in doing so, give up an important part of themselves.

In CFFT, however, with the aid of the therapist, family members can learn to tell their **core truths** to other members in a non-defensive, non-blaming, heartfelt way including the use of "I" statements and with an attempt to take responsibility for their share of the difficulties. This allows for the creation and expression of more compassion between the family members, and greatly reduces the amount of guilt and shame.

When the communication goes beyond blaming and complaining and becomes softer and deeper, it also becomes more real and authentic. In effect, the therapist helps to bridge the chasms that have built up through many years of hurt and misunderstanding in the entire family. Family members are given the opportunity to get to know each other in a new way, based on who each one is when they allow themselves to be fully in contact with self and other. Healing and growth can then begin to progress in an upward spiral rather than continue the negative spiral that has resulted in so much pain and distance over the years.

As people begin to share their core truths with one another, not only do their interpersonal relationships change, but major shifts also begin to filter through to their own sense of **personal identity.** Thus, one discovers important things about oneself through one's interactions with others. As Harry Stack Sullivan pointed out in his Interpersonal Theory (1), so much of who we are is a consequence of who we are with other people. Nowhere is this more pronounced than with one's family members. When a person is courageous enough to finally speak his truth to his family members, he can also see who he is when he is not giving up a part of himself to protect other family members. Consequently, he becomes freer from the entanglement with his family, less tied to old roles and patterns, and more able to make healthy decisions about the kind and extent of emotional involvement he wants to have with them.

In cases of severe emotional, physical, and sexual abuse by parents, an adult child may realize the wisdom of setting and/or keeping appropriate boundaries around time and place and frequency of meetings with the parent(s), while not cutting off from them entirely. Rather than striving for "increased togetherness" in every family, the goal of CFFT is for members to be more honest with one another, letting each other know where they stand in relation to one another, and defining a structure for the continuing relationship.

Learning these skills of deep and honest communication within one's own family of origin also allows family members to have more insight and clarity in their other relationships outside the family, as well as with their own partners and offspring. In this way, CFFT allows for **intergenerational** healing to occur. Insights gained in CFFT sessions are easily transferable to situations involving friends, work associates and other people who enter our lives.

2.
Qualities of the CFFT Therapist

The CFFT therapist must be able to embody qualities of sensitivity, empathy, and attunement to other's feelings, while being authentic, direct, and not afraid of telling the truth as she sees it. She is a model for the family of being comfortable in herself, taking risks, valuing depth in communication, and seeing the humor and the paradoxes of being human. In CFFT, the therapist, as well as the family, continues to grow, thus making the work alive and exciting for both.

Authenticity

Since authentic interpersonal involvement is so crucial to this approach, the therapist models her own authentic expression of feelings with the family. Although sometimes taking charge of the sessions in a very "expert" way, the therapist does her best to create a balance between her therapeutic role and that of an "I-thou" relationship (2) with family members. She is not afraid to reveal her own feelings at appropriate times.

The therapist invites people to be *themselves*, by being *herself*. Rather than inappropriate self-disclosure, the therapist is attempting to be genuine about how she is feeling in the moment. This helps to create a container wherein self-exploration among family members is made more possible. By promoting authenticity and self-expressiveness in the family members and within the therapist herself, this model helps to free clients from rigid family rules and roles, and allows them to become more expansive in the ways they can interact with each other. Bringing her own energy and personality into the work, the therapist can be a source of inspiration and a model for the family members. With each new family, a new relationship is forged so that the therapist, as well as the family members, never stop growing. Being with families in this way keeps the work alive, fresh, exciting, and growthful. The therapist learns *with* her clients so that "burn-out" is less likely to occur. As in many other experiential therapies, such as Gestalt, CFFT is based on the idea that human growth is achieved through the quality of contact we have with others.

Focus on the Core

CFFT has been described as "going for the love" or looking for the feelings beneath the words. One assumption of this method is that love, or the desire to connect, is often a common feeling underlying many kinds of family interactions, and that a great deal of pain and suffering has gotten in the way of individual family members feeling and expressing that love for one another. Typically, families avoid talking about the issues that have come between them and that is a primary reason why they are experiencing conflict.

In CFFT, the therapist attempts to find these common desires for connection between family members and to point them out. She helps to build bridges where communication has broken down, by encouraging each family member to get to a deeper and more vulnerable place in himself or herself and in relation to the other. Healing can only come from a place of honesty and vulnerability, which is the basis of this approach. Family members are often awestruck when they discover their own heretofore hidden truths and express them to their loved ones.

Thus, the goal of CFFT is to help each family member communicate honestly and directly with one another, from their hearts as well as their heads. The therapist is trying to create an environment where the family members can hear each other, get things off their chests, communicate directly, and express themselves more fully than they have been able to do before. The hope is that by expressing their core fears and longings to one another in a deeply honest and connected way, the family members can start to rebuild their feelings of trust for one another and will eventually be able to have more joy, aliveness, spontaneity, and depth in their relationships. This transformation can be seen to occur even in deeply dysfunctional families.

Truth

On the other hand, the CFFT therapist is also "going for the truth." She is not afraid to be frank, to say what she sees going on in the family, and to call the dynamics as she sees them. Her candor about this impacts family members with a sense of their core interpersonal truths in the family. This, in turn, evokes vulnerable emotional states that allow for significant healing to occur in the moment. When the unspoken rules are finally spoken, the stagnant relationships uncovered, and the triangulations exposed, family members are able to engage with one another with a newfound freedom that would have been impossible before. In essence, the therapist is helping to **empower** family members to be their **whole selves** in relation to those closest to them.

While some schools of family therapy focus on rebuilding love among family members and others focus on therapists being more candid and/or confrontational, CFFT tries to incorporate both of these aspects of therapy, the yin and the yang. Thus, the CFFT therapist must be capable of having deep empathy and compassion for family members and, out of this compassion, be able to speak her truth as she sees it. Having natural grace in being direct is a helpful quality for the CFFT therapist to embody. Hopefully, through her modeling of this wholeness in her communications with them, family members can learn to be both loving and truthful with one another.

Empathy

By definition, empathy is "the capacity for participating in another's feelings or thoughts." The German word for empathy, *einfuhlung*, means "feeling into." The CFFT therapist feels into the feelings and ideas of the family members. She intentionally lets her boundaries become a bit more permeable with a view to letting in and soaking up just a little bit of each one of the family members with whom she is communicating. She needs to sense what each member is trying to express and ask questions or reflect their words in such a way that they feel heard and understood by her. Once this happens, the family member feels validated and can begin to express his core feelings and ideas to other members, with the eventual goal of relating empathically with one another without the therapist there to guide them.

Sensitivity and Attunement

The therapist using CFFT must have a high level of sensitivity to the feeling states of the individuals in the family, and to the energy of the family as a whole. She enters the session with an openness of heart and mind, and allows the family to present whatever in that moment needs to be the focus and potential catalyst for change. The therapist working in this model is a verbal minimalist, speaking only when necessary. She is not there to take center stage, but observes carefully what is happening with the family until her interventions are needed and can be utilized in the best way possible.

Listening to Language

One way that the CFFT therapist picks up on the feeling states of the family members is by listening very closely to their use of language. Oftentimes a member will start to say something to another member and then fear will obstruct the flow of what he has begun to say. He may start to backpedal or sugarcoat what he is saying or go off on another tangent. Those are times when the therapist can take him back to his original statement by just uttering the last word he said before going in another direction. This gentle kind of intervention can help steer the family member back to the feeling he was expressing before the fear took over and help him to take the risk that he had spontaneously begun to take. The existential psychotherapist, Clark Moustakas, put it this way:

> Words invite us to enter into the life of another and create new directions for our own living. Language lifts out and delivers over what would otherwise remain hidden. It makes possible liberation of thoughts and feelings, and frees one from habits and relationships that interfere with self-fulfillment. Language discloses the way things are and reveals what has been concealed. (3)

While empathy, sensitive attunement, and listening are listed separately here, in reality they are all interrelated. Thus, if one is sensitively attuned and listens attentively, he is then in a position to "feel into," or empathize with, what is going on for the client.

Humor

Because family therapy can be a frightening endeavor for most families to engage in, it is important that the sessions allow for some humor to balance out the seriousness of the situation. As the therapist and family get to know each other better, they will discover the extent to which humor, lightness, or playfulness can be a part of the sessions. It is important for all to keep in mind that even though the family is experiencing some difficult times, they are still capable of keeping their perspective, and that laughing together at certain moments can be very healing as well. As Bugenthal has described, "Humor in sessions is not a product of conscious intent to be funny on the part of the therapist (or the family members) but grows out of their serious and total involvement with the task at hand. Genuine humor comes out of a deeper fountain of being in touch with the paradoxes and surprises of life." (4)

Analytical Mind

Because much of family therapy is detective work, it helps for the CFFT therapist to have an analytical mind. It is important to be able to quickly grasp the various dynamics in the family and to verbalize them when it is appropriate to do so. Much of this work is done in short-term settings, so the sooner the therapist has an idea of what may be going on in the family, the sooner she can test out this hypothesis with them. The nature of family therapy is such that there is a great deal to pay attention to in any given moment. Having a facility with creating and exploring hypotheses about the family's dynamics will stand her in good stead using this method, as she will be quicker to sort out what may seem to be a very chaotic situation.

3.
Relationship to Other Schools of Family Therapy

As an experiential approach, CFFT takes much of its inspiration from Carl Whitaker and the Gestalt therapists. However, a good understanding of Murray Bowen's and Salvador Minuchin's ideas will help the practitioner to understand conceptually where many of the basic family therapy ideas originated and can be helpful in getting a broader view of what is transpiring in the family. CFFT is unique in the way that it integrates parts of all of these approaches and results in a method that is both deep in its focus and short-term in its application. This book attempts to translate what may look like "magic" into a step-by-step process that is not that difficult to learn.

Historical Perspective

Historically, we can see where the separation between individual and family therapy began. Sigmund Freud (1856-1939) was the first one to get interested in the family drama. In his theory of the Oedipus and Electra complexes, he stressed the importance of the interaction between family members, the hidden passions that, though largely unconscious, had such an important effect on the adult personalities that were to later develop.

The fatal error for Freud was that he believed that the most important aspects of these family dramas were to be studied through the dreams and fantasies, the intrapsychic life, of his patients, i.e. through the psychoanalytic method. What he failed to realize was the importance of the *actual* relationships his patients were having with their families, and the benefit that could be derived from having these people dialogue with one another directly. Thus, the actual family context had become irrelevant to Freud because, whatever was thought to be curative in the therapy (namely the dreams and fantasies of his patients) was already recorded in the patient's mind and could be analyzed in the individual psychoanalytic session. Freud not only *neglected* this significant aspect of his patient's life — he outright *rejected* it — believing that seeing other family members of his patients would *interfere with the transference,* one of the major techniques of psychoanalysis. Thus, the family was shut out of individual therapy, and with that a major portion of a patient's *real life* problems were no longer under investigation.

Freud's paradigm of "individual therapy" was enormously influential for mental health workers throughout the first half of the 20th century, and is still very important today. It took the work of Alfred Adler, Harry Stack Sullivan, Murray Bowen, Don Jackson, and, most prominently, Nathan Ackerman, to break from this paradigm and put the "Family Therapy" paradigm on the map. In 1958, Ackerman wrote the first major book in the field, entitled *The Psychodynamics of Family Life* (5), in which he discussed his recognition that the problems of one member of a family could not be understood apart from those of other family members. His "unique" form of treatment was to see the whole family at once in order to discern the *interactional* patterns that were giving rise to an individual in a family presenting a symptom. This individual was given the name "identified patient" or IP, suggesting that s/he was merely identified as the patient because s/he manifested a symptom, when in truth it was the whole family that was really "the patient." It was Ackerman's writings and therapeutic work with families that finally opened the door for this new paradigm to surface among mental health practitioners. His approach included seeing the family as a system, with one person's pain or difficult behavior being directly related to dysfunctional relationships within the whole family. Consequently, entire families now began coming to the consulting room together to explore their actual relationships with one another, in hopes of resolving family conflicts.

Grounded in Experiential Therapy

CFFT is **experiential** in that it is concerned with the quality of how things are experienced by different family members in the present moment. Rather than employing a set of techniques, this approach is more oriented to what happens in the relationships between the therapist and the family members, as well as among the family members themselves.

One assumption of **experiential** therapy, as practiced by Carl Whitaker (6), is that personal growth occurs only in the relational experience, and depends mainly on the **person** of the therapist, regardless of his or her orientation to therapy. It is believed that it is in this intimate relationship that the clients learn to redevelop a natural capacity to explore and grow, which they can practice immediately with other members of the family. The **core learning** which occurs is the increased ability for being intimate in relationship, i.e. being able to express oneself and open oneself to new experience when in relationship with others to whom one is close. Family members, who work together in the CFFT process, find themselves able to relate more intimately with each other as well as have an increased sense of presence, self-responsibility, personal freedom, authenticity, and reciprocity.

Gestalt Family Therapy

Similar to **Gestalt** Family Therapy, as practiced by Virginia Satir (7) and Walter Kempler (8), in CFFT the therapist is attempting to help family members learn to identify and communicate what they feel and need from one another in the most *specific* terms possible, and to try to get these needs met in the family. This often requires going beyond old familiar roles, taking emotional risks, and saying what they have not had the courage to say before. Doing this helps family members free themselves from the often-unconscious binds they have been locked into in the family and encourages them to take charge of their own lives.

The use of **"I" statements**, which encourage individuation, heightens the emotional intensity within the family. Working in the **here-and-now**, this method focuses on the potential for healing in the present and possibilities for the future. Also, as in Gestalt therapy, the CFFT therapist encourages family members to be aware not only of *what* they are saying, but also of *how* they are saying it, going on the Gestalt principle that awareness, in and of itself, can be curative. (9) In keeping with the use of **immediate contact,** family members are directed to speak with one another rather than to the therapist.

Bowenian Family Therapy

Unlike some experiential and Gestalt therapists, the practitioner of CFFT *does* utilize concepts and methods from non-experiential approaches. Her thinking is informed by **Bowen's** family therapy, in terms of looking at **intergenerational** patterns that weave through families over time, **triangulation,** influence of **sibling position,** and **differentiation of Self**. (10)

In regard to the differentiation process, which Bowen addresses at length, the CFFT therapist is facilitating family members to identify and express their **core interpersonal truths** based on their thoughts as well as their feelings. Unlike solely feeling-based therapies, CFFT acknowledges that a **modulation of affect** is sometimes necessary in order to get people to think clearly and see what is really going on in the system in which they are enmeshed. Oftentimes, the system has felt so confusing to them because they are overly entangled in its grasp. Thus, getting distance and objectivity in regard to the family is a significant aspect of CFFT.

Minuchin's Structural Family Therapy

Practitioners of CFFT conceptualize and put into action the altering of boundaries and realigning of **subsystems** when appropriate. They would also find the concepts of **enmeshed** and **disengaged** families to be helpful. CFFT therapists would be open to seeing particular subsystems of the family alone if this seemed desirable.

Finally, CFFT's use of the **direct interaction** has similarities to Minuchin's technique of **enactment.** (11)

Uniqueness of Core Focused Family Therapy

While CFFT draws from and builds on these other schools of family therapy, it is unique in the way they are integrated into one approach. The emphasis on encouraging family members to go directly to their **core interpersonal truths**, to where the deep, unsaid, unsayable truths lie hidden from the individual himself, as well as from his family members, makes this approach both deep and time-efficient. The healing occurs when one has acknowledged those truths to oneself and expressed them to significant family members. When the unsayable things become sayable and said, and the relationship is adjusted accordingly, the presenting symptom is no longer needed. Because both analysis and intuition are major tools of the CFFT process, **core issues** can be gotten to relatively quickly so that long-term therapy is not often necessary.

Capturing the Magic

One criticism of some experiential approaches to family therapy is that they seem more like art than science. The lack of explicit techniques and the emphasis on the personality, intuition, and experience of the therapist, combine to make these methods seem more like *magic* than a predictable and scientific body of knowledge.

While the authors acknowledge that there is definitely an art to practicing Core Focused Family Therapy, they believe that after thoroughly digesting this book, the clinician will have a good sense of how this approach works and how they can put it into practice with their clients. Section II gives a step-by-step analysis of this method from the first phone call to the termination of family treatment. The transcripts from actual family sessions peppered throughout this section provide a flavor of the work, which should help the clinician to get more of an intuitive understanding of how the method is utilized in real life. After reading this book, the clinician can begin to conceptualize and practice CFFT, and with time and experience, begin to *"capture their own magic"* in their work with clients.

4.
Overview of General Principles in Family Therapy

Entering the world of family therapy causes a radical shift for the clinician who is used to practicing individual therapy. Whereas in the latter, the therapist meets one person whose "story" he listens to and tries to understand and empathize with, in family therapy, the therapist is exposed to a minimum of two but perhaps as many as four, five, or six different perspectives regarding the same situation. As in Akira Kurosawa's classic movie, *Rashomon*, which presents three different sides of a story from the three different perspectives of the characters, the viewer or therapist is often left to his own devices to find out which one, if any, is the "real" one.

This can pose quite a predicament for a therapist who is being sought after to "solve" the family's problem. Whom should she believe? Or is there some truth to all of their perspectives? Such a dilemma can understandably be threatening to a therapist who has not been exposed to the family therapy paradigm. One goal of this book is to help interested professionals in the mental health field, and students of psychotherapy, to become less confused and intimidated by the prospect of "seeing the whole family." After reading this book, the student or professional will hopefully have an easier time making the shift from the classic individual therapy paradigm to the family systems approach, and to CFFT in particular. Furthermore, those people considering bringing their whole family into therapy will have a better idea of what they can expect to experience when they get there.

The Identified Patient (IP)

It is crucial for the clinician working with families to grasp the notion of the family being a system, and to believe in this way of thinking despite apparent evidence to the contrary. A family often comes into treatment as the result of a particular child getting into trouble at home, at school, or out in the world. The family may enter therapy prepared to get help for this child, wedded to the idea that the other relationships in the family are unrelated to the issues going on for the IP. It is the therapist's job to get the family to see the broader context in which the IP's symptoms exist, to expand the **surface area** of the problem. If the family is narrowly focused on the IP as the problem, then the therapist must artfully shift the focus toward the family system as a whole. It is important that she do this in a subtle and gentle way, since many families truly believe that the problem is with the IP alone. The more resistant the family members are to seeing that they, too, are part of the problem, the harder it will be to get them to consider other ways of looking at the family problems. Thus, the therapist needs to be careful about not pushing her perspective too forcefully, as that may cause family members to become defensive, and they may not come back to therapy. It has been said that the goal of the first session is for the family to return for the second session.

Dispelling the Myth of the IP

One way to break up the notion of the IP is to bring attention to the different relationships in the family. By asking what else is going on in the family, aside from with the IP, the therapist can learn about different emotional alignments in the family system. Let us take the example of a family coming into therapy stating that they are here because of Jonathan's misbehavior at school. If the therapist then asks the mother, "Well, how are things going with you and Jane (Jonathan's sister)?" the reply might be, "Well, actually, I never see her enough." That could be the therapist's opportunity to get the mom to explore her relationship with Jane further by saying, "Well, tell me about not seeing her enough." This may lead the conversation away from being focused on Jonathan (the IP), and more toward other family issues. The goal here is to try to increase the surface area of the problem, and to broaden the family's perspective on what really constitutes this family's problem.

Another way to dispel "the family myth of the IP" is to give space to the therapist's "allies" to talk about other problem areas that may be going on in the family. Often the parents are the ones who believe most in the centrality of the IP's role as the problem. When the whole family is asked what other issues exist in the family, it will often be the siblings that are forthcoming about other difficulties. One of the children may say, "I feel like my dad is always busy working." Another may say, "My mom is always nagging me."

The therapist can use this alignment of the **sibling subsystem** (12) to her advantage, because it naturally forces the parents to look at the possibility of alternatives to the central theme of the IP as the problem. Not only does the alignment of the sibling subsystem "blow the parents cover," but it also helps the IP. Because the family has scapegoated the IP for so long, he himself often believes that the family problems are entirely his fault. But if the IP begins to hear that his siblings also have problems with the parents or with each other, then he may begin to feel more "normal" and more bonded with his siblings, which will help to rebuild his sense of self-esteem.

For example, a family consisting of two parents and three adult children comes to their first family therapy session saying they are here because the youngest son, Jason, has a drug problem. In the check-in (which will be discussed in detail later in this book), both parents are adamant that the only problem in the family is Jason's drug use. Even Jason agrees that the family is there because of him. In other words, Jason himself has bought into the idea that he is the IP. When the oldest son, Mike, gets to check in, he asserts that "ostensibly" the family is in therapy for Jason, but that he, Mike, believes there are a lot of other problems in the family. When asked to give an example of what he means, Mike replies, "I feel like I'm always trying to measure up to my dad's expectations, but always coming up short." In the daughter Josie's check-in, she says, "As I think of it, my relationship with Mom has been strained for some time now."

This then gives the therapist an opportunity to broaden the **surface area** of the problem beyond the IP. The therapist can gently say to the parents, "I know you came here for your youngest son, Jason (the IP), but we've heard from both your other children, and they are feeling uncomfortable about other aspects of the family relationships. It seems like there is more going on in this family than just your youngest son's drug problems."

By providing these alternative points of view about the nature of the family's issues, these other family members can be seen as "allies" of the therapist. In their willingness to open up about some of the more hidden aspects of the family's functioning, they begin to catalyze a more thorough exploration into the dynamics of the family system. If the parents still insist that there are no other problems, it may be necessary to accept their point of view for a while until further trust in you as the therapist is established or as more evidence comes to the fore from other family members. If the parents remain rigid about this, it may be necessary to go along with and discuss the problem with the IP as they see it.

It can also be conceptualized that the IP is "holding a certain emotion" for the family such as anger, sadness, fear, or hurt, and that until other members take responsibility for their own difficult emotions, it will be hard to free the IP from his role as scapegoat. Scapegoating turns out to be "convenient" for the other family members, who often prefer to think of the problem as residing outside of themselves.

The Johnson family came in for treatment about a year after the parents had divorced. Custody was determined such that the three children, aged 8, 13, and 16 were frequently shuttling back and forth between living at the mom's house and the dad's house. One of the presenting problems revolved around the 8-year-old girl, Melissa, who was exhibiting temper tantrums whenever she couldn't find a garment that she wanted to wear. Others in the family seemed to be more accepting of the new arrangement. On further examination, however, it became clear that all of the members were having reactions to the chaos that had ensued since the parental break-up, and that Melissa had been "elected" by the family to "act out" the feelings of insecurity, confusion, and anger. Once the other family members were able to acknowledge their own discomfort around living in two different homes, Melissa was freed up from her role as the IP.

Shift from Individual to Family Paradigm

The shift from the "individual paradigm" to the "family paradigm" is a dynamic one. Instead of focusing on one individual, we are now focusing not only on a greater number of people, but also on the different permutations and combinations that their relationships create, as well as looking at the system as a whole. Thus, we have gone from a narrow picture to a greatly expanded one in terms of what is causing stress in the family.

When the family comes in saying it is just the IP who is having problems, they are continuing to see things from a narrow perspective. The therapist must help them to increase the **surface area** with which to view the problem. In the first case described above, the attempt is to expand the parents' view of the problem from solely Jason's drug use to other themes in the family: pressure, expectation, isolation, and lack of communication among all the family members, even the parents' own relationship with each other. This last piece is often the most difficult to address, since, to many people, the prospect of problems in their intimate relationship is very threatening to their personal and family security. In fact, it is often the case that because the parents are so reluctant to look at their own relationship problems, a child may consciously or unconsciously "take the heat off" of them by becoming symptomatic.

Homeostasis

This leads us to another crucial concept in family dynamics, **homeostasis.** If we look at a family as a living system, we can see a set of contradictory forces that affect all family members. On the one hand, there is the homeostatic force that causes things to remain the same in spite of external pressures that are pushing for change. On the other hand, there is a growth force that is directed toward growth and change. In the course of a family's life cycle, change is always occurring as children and adults go through various developmental stages. It is usually at these times of transition into a more difficult stage that the family will seek help. In family therapy terms, the "homeostatic balance" is being threatened, anxiety is mounting, and someone in the family will try, consciously or unconsciously, to prevent this situation from getting any worse by acting out or becoming symptomatic in some way.

For instance, one couple may work very well together when an infant is born but, when the child becomes a toddler, they may run into more difficulty in their attempts to discipline him. Other families will struggle more when the last child goes off to school and mom, feeling the "empty nest," begins to demand more from her husband. Still other families will get into difficulty when the children become adolescents and the parents' own unresolved issues from that period are activated.

While the couple clearly wants help for their child who is exhibiting problems, they are often less aware of or less focused on the strain in their own relationship. In fact, it is often the case that the child's problems are bringing the parents together in a new way that, though not ultimately desirable, is still preferable to the growing distance both had felt earlier. Thus, we could say that the child's problematic behavior is serving the homeostatic function of forcing the parents to come together to try to solve the child's problem, whereas the absence of the problematic behavior could lead to more extreme distance and separation in the parents' relationship.

Once again, we see the IP "taking the heat off" the parents' troubled relationship by giving them a project to work on together (the child's troubling behavior), which, though a sacrifice for the child, is helping to maintain the family homeostasis. Going to a therapist at this point can spark the growth force in the family so that parents can begin to look at their own relationship and the child doesn't have to sacrifice himself any longer.

If a couple does not come to terms with their own difficulties in their relationship, even though the original IP has shown individual progress in his behavior, another child in the family may begin showing new symptoms and, in essence, become a second IP. Thus, the symptoms can bounce back and forth among the offspring because the deep-rooted issues have not yet been explored and resolved in the family.

Safe Container

Because these relationship issues are so potentially threatening to a family, the therapist must provide a **safe container** in which the family can take a good, honest look at themselves and each other and see what they are willing to change in order to reach a higher level of functioning. Doing this requires that the therapist be fair, empathic, and understanding, yet be willing to "rock the boat" with a family once some measure of trust is established. Some family patterns may be maintained vociferously by some family members and must be challenged if the family is to make positive shifts. On the other hand, if the therapist is too aggressive, cold, or pushy, it is likely to backfire, and the family will leave therapy. The therapist's sense of **timing** is crucial in this work. She must know when to push and when to support, when the family needs her help and when they are doing fine on their own.

Length of Treatment

Family therapy is traditionally of a shorter duration than individual therapy and CFFT is known, too, for its short-term usage. Because the family can practice the gains they are making with each other during the week, changes can often occur more rapidly. Typically, a family is seen for one-and-a-half to two hours per session, and the sessions may occur every week, every other week, or even once a month. The frequency will depend on the family's needs and preferences as well as how well they are integrating what they are learning in the sessions.

While some families are highly motivated to reach a deeper communication level with each other and may continue the treatment for several years, other families who are looking for relief from immediate stresses may stay for only three to six months and leave after some basic changes are made. Even just one or a few sessions of CFFT can be very helpful for some families who work well on their own and just need a therapist to point out areas to focus on.

Section II

CFFT Practice

5.
Therapist Preparation

One of the most important things a therapist must do before she actually sees a family in therapy is to have considerable awareness of the dynamics in her own family. It is important not to be sucked into the client family's dynamics or you may be doing more harm than good. At the very least, it is essential to have a supervisor or therapist with whom you discuss whether you are the right person to see this family and, once in treatment with them, to help you to navigate between which issues are yours and which are theirs.

Areas of Competence

Each family therapist will develop different areas of expertise in working with families based on interest, experience, and possibly personal familiarity with a particular kind of problem. For instance, if the therapist is a parent herself and feels knowledgeable about child rearing at various ages on the developmental spectrum, she may be inclined to see a family with young children. Another therapist, who has worked in a psychiatric hospital, may feel comfortable working with a severely disturbed family member who is currently on medication.

On the other hand, a therapist who has come from a very violent family may choose NOT to see a family where physical violence is a key issue. It is important, as a family therapist, to be aware of your own areas of prejudice and **counter-transference**. Some therapists have received special training in working with chemical dependency in families and enjoy this kind of work. They may have originally come from an alcoholic family and feel they have gained enough insight from their own personal work to be very helpful with such families. Other therapists, who have had considerable experience with trauma and loss in their life, may feel comfortable working with families with a member who has a terminal illness.

The key to deciding whether or not to work with a family is past experience. If you have never worked with a particular population before, and you are interested in doing so, it is best to have a consultant to help you with the family. This can be a colleague, a mentor, or anyone you know who has had experience in doing this kind of work. It is not a good idea to experiment with a new population on your own. If you are unskillful with the family, you may turn them off to the whole idea of family therapy, thus making it unlikely that they will seek help from any family therapist again. This would obviously be a very unfortunate outcome.

Counter-Transference

When a therapist has major unresolved issues with her own family of origin, it can be dangerous for her to work with entire families. If she grew up caretaking her father, blaming her mother, or envying her older brother, she can easily project these issues onto the family she is working with in therapy. Since there is often so much happening at once in family therapy, it would be easy for such a therapist to inadvertently take on one of these familiar roles.

For example, in a family in which everyone is scapegoating dad who, in fact, does seem to be a difficult person, it would be easy for the therapist who still has many unresolved feelings of anger towards her own father, to jump in and join the bandwagon with the family against the dad. It is thus very important for any therapist working with families to have done extensive work with her own family of origin. While this work may have occurred in individual therapy, it is particularly helpful if the therapist herself has been in therapy with her own family of origin or nuclear family. In some family therapy training programs, it is possible to simulate family therapy sessions with one's own family through the use of **Psychodramatic Family Therapy** (discussed in Section III).

While we have already mentioned the power of the family to "induce" behaviors in their children (e.g., making a child feel guilty, ashamed, etc.), it should be noted that the family is also capable of "inducing" behaviors in the therapist. For instance, they may unconsciously try to make the therapist into a rescuer, a failure, a fool, or a sage. It need not be the result of the therapist's own counter-transference that she takes on this role, but more of the family's need to put her there. In any case, the clearer the therapist is about the destructive potential of such inductions in working with the family, the more likely she is to recognize that she has been selected to play a particular role. Often with the help of a consultant, she can extricate herself from this position and be more aware of the situation the next time it occurs.

6.
Selecting Clients and Setting up Appointments

Family therapy begins with the first phone contact. It is important even at the first moment of contact to remain neutral and objective, but not cold or matter of fact when discussing the family with the person who made the call. Encouraging all members to come in for at least the first session will make the therapy a lot easier. How to handle situations when the whole family is not available or willing to come to the session depends on the particular family circumstances.

Pre-Initial-Session Interactions

When a family member calls to schedule their first family therapy appointment, it is helpful for the therapist to ask that family member an open-ended question such as, "Tell me a little about what's going on in the family." If the family member presents the problem and lays all the blame on the Identified Patient (IP), then it is advisable to keep the discussion to a minimum. The therapist does not want to encourage the family member that is calling to believe that the family problem is just about the IP. However, if the family member is giving a balanced introduction to the family problems, then it can be useful to talk for a few minutes to try to understand what the presenting problem is and who is involved in it. The therapist should keep the conversation to a minimum, perhaps five minutes.

It is important for the therapist to take notes on this first phone call and put them in the case notebook in which she will keep all the ongoing notes of the family sessions. Included in the intake information are the names and ages of all the family members, the fee set for this family, the address and phone number of the caller, and the time set for the first appointment. If the family member mentions any symptoms, acts of violence, chemical dependency issues, or strengths of the family members, this should also appear in the notes.

If, after listening to the family member, the therapist feels this is a case she can work with, she can indicate that to the family member and set up an appointment. The therapist wants most of the work to happen in the session, not on the phone, and not from just one person's point of view. If the therapist does not feel qualified to see this family, she may give the family member names of other therapists who might be more appropriate.

What if the family member who calls about an appointment asks the therapist about his/her approach to family therapy? The therapist can say, "The first thing we do is find out what each person's perspective is on how the family functions, and what each family member's concerns are. The ultimate goal is to help the family members get to a point where they can hear each other and communicate what they haven't been able to say on their own, in an honest and direct way."

Who Should Come to the First Session?

If the family is living as a unit, it is very important for all the members of that unit to attend the first session. If, for example, the mother in a family tells you that she could never get her husband to come in, that is an indication of one of the possible problems in the family. If you were to see the mother and children without the husband, you would be reinforcing the present dynamics in the family, which may be that mother is over-involved and father is under-involved in the family's problems.

It is a good idea to emphasize how necessary it is to have the father there and to suggest that he call the therapist on his own if he has some concerns about coming. Often the mother is afraid to press the father to come, but when she has the therapist's support, she can more easily confront the issue of the joint handling of family problems. If the particular child that the parent expresses concern about is younger than age five, it may be better to refer the family to a therapist with an expertise in working with young children.

With a family of adult children living in their own homes, it is also a good idea to have the whole family attend the first session. If it is too difficult to bring the entire family together, such as when one of the members is in another part of the country, then it may be necessary to proceed with whichever family members are currently living locally. In cases where a grandparent, aunt, or uncle is an everyday part of this family's life, they can be included in the session, too.

Other factors to consider in deciding who should come to the first session are the therapist's comfort with larger groups of people and the size of the therapist's office. It is generally a good idea to begin with all the family members present and then, when appropriate, to have **subsystems** of the family return for later sessions. For example, if the work starts to become more focused on the parents, and they are uncomfortable talking about their sexual intimacy in front of their children, it may be wise to see the couple alone for some sessions before seeing the entire family again. Indeed, there are different schools of thought on how much to discuss sexuality or money matters with children present. While some therapists such as Whitaker and Napier (13) would encourage *all* family members to be present during such discussions, Minuchin (14) would emphasize the need for clear boundaries between the spousal and sibling subsystems. The authors of CFFT believe that the therapist must be very sensitive to the boundary and privacy issues for the parents and to respect their needs when determining what is talked about in sessions. Certainly the parents should not be shamed in any way for insisting on such boundaries.

It might also be fruitful for the therapist to work alone with the sibling subsystem at some point if she sees that they are having trouble expressing themselves in front of the parents. The intention would be to get the whole family group together again at a later session.

In practice, it is not usually the case that a whole family calls to come to therapy. Family therapy may have been suggested to the family by the school, the church, or even the police, and that is why they have come. It may also be that the therapist is seeing an individual client who wants to bring his whole family into the sessions for a few meetings. This is particularly true when the parent(s) live in another city or state and are planning a visit with the client. Or it could be that the individual client feels ready to approach his parents now and would like the support of the therapist to do that. If the therapist and the family agree to have these meetings, it should be with the stated goal of helping all concerned to understand what is going on with the individual client. If the problem were about the system or about any of the other individual members of the system, it would be better to refer them to another family or couples therapist. If the client wants to begin regular family sessions with his family rather than just a few exploratory sessions, it is best to have the whole family begin therapy with another family therapist while the original therapist continues doing individual work with the client.

Of course, the therapist doing even a few sessions with the client and his family should have training in family therapy before agreeing to work with the whole family. She should be especially cautious during the session about any tendency to side with the parents against her individual client, since this could easily create a feeling of betrayal and mistrust in her client. Her loyalty clearly needs to be to her individual client in this context, whereas in regular family work the therapist's goal is to be impartial and to represent all family members equally.

7.
The Check-In

The check-in is your first opportunity to make contact with each person in the family. While it may be tempting to get more into the "meat" of the family dynamics when someone in the family begins to argue with another one's check-in, it is important to keep the boundary around each person's share. In order for any group to be cohesive, the first task is for each person to feel included. The check-in provides that sense of safety from which trust can begin to develop.

Introducing Yourself in the Session

At the beginning of the session, the therapist does not need to do much of an introduction of herself, her training, or of the process of family therapy, unless the family members request this specifically. The therapist has already talked with one member of the family on the phone when he called to set up the first appointment. The therapist can begin by saying: "My name is…and I guess I spoke with you on the phone (while making eye contact with the family member that originally called). I'd like to get to know each of you more and find out what brings you here and how you see what's going on in the family." Then it is time to move on to the check-in with each person.

Check-In

At this initial stage of the session, the dialogue is solely between the therapist and a given family member. This is in contrast to the **direct interactions** that take place between two family members and will be discussed later in the book.

The check-in questions should be deep enough to get at least an initial sense of who the person is, what they want, how cooperative they will be, what their resources are, and what their energy is like. Of course, as the sessions continue, the therapist will find out more about each family member and about the relationships among the various members. Another thing to look for in the check-in is information on the dynamics in the family.

The therapist should take careful note to see what the **alliances** are in the family as well as the **coalitions**. Thus, she should look for clues about which members seem to see eye to eye on issues, stick up for each other, and make non-verbal gestures of agreement with one another. As a corollary, the therapist should also be looking for which people seem to be antagonistic towards each other, in disagreement with or critical of one another, or give non-verbal signals of agitation with the other.

The practitioner should be noticing who takes what role in the family, e.g., who is in pain; who gets angry easily; who is the martyr; who is the "identified patient"; who is the caretaker; who acts polite and reserved; who plays out being the disinterested, non-committal one; who tells it like it is; which one is confused; who is the spokesperson; etc.

Another salient function of the check-in is in its message to the family that in therapy the emphasis will be on communication of feelings. By speaking only to the therapist and not to other family members at this stage, they can experience "feeling talk" in a less threatening way. So, in a sense, the check-in is a warm-up to the direct interaction that will come next. In this way, the check-in serves a training/modeling function for the family sessions.

Who Begins the Check-In?

To begin the check-in, the therapist usually asks, "Who wants to start us off?" By doing this, rather than asking a particular person to begin, the therapist can see who the spokesperson for the family is. On the other hand, if the therapist has spoken to the mom on the phone already, she may be more inclined to begin her questioning with the dad.

Every family therapy session includes a check-in at the beginning. However, during the first session the therapist needs to spend extra time on the check-in to find out why the family is entering therapy and begin to bond with each member of the family. An important task in the first session is for the therapist to identify what each of the family members sees as the reason the family has come in for therapy.

For example, one family member may summarize the situation by saying, "We're here because we're feeling disconnected and we're struggling to communicate with each other." while another may say, "We're here because Lisa keeps getting in trouble." Each person in the family may see the problem a little bit differently and it is important to be aware of these differences.

Three Main Areas in Check-In

There are three main areas of questioning in the check-in that the therapist should cover with each family member before moving on to the next person. They are as follows:

1. Basic Information

Gather information about occupation, marital status, number of dependents, and grade in school.

From an adult the therapist might ask

- What do you do for work?
- Do you enjoy what you do?
- Where and with whom do you live?
- Are you married?

- Do you have children?

For a child, the therapist might want to know

- What grade are you in at school?
- What do you like to do for fun?

The therapist uses these questions as an opportunity to get to know and develop a connection with each individual person in the family.

Here is an example of the therapist beginning the check-in with the father in a family of adult children: (Note: All examples in this manual are taken from transcripts of real family sessions that the primary author has conducted.)

> Therapist: So, Bill, it sounds like you want to start us off. What do you do for work?
>
> Bill: I'm a lawyer.
>
> Therapist: Oh, how is that for you?

Here is an example of the therapist checking-in with an adult son:

> Therapist: And how about you, Tom? Where do you live?
>
> Tom: Actually, I live in Richmond.
>
> Therapist: Are you married?
>
> Tom: I am.
>
> Therapist: And do you have kids?
>
> Tom: Yes…two little ones.
>
> Therapist: And what is it that you do?

2. "Here-and-Now" Questions

Try to find out what it is like for each person to be in therapy today with his or her family.

Here is an example of the therapist checking-in with an adult daughter:

Therapist: So Miranda, what's it like for you to be here today with your family?

Miranda: Well, I'm a little nervous but kind of interested to hear what everyone has to say.

Therapist: So, nervous, but curious as well?

Another way the therapist can approach this question is:

Therapist [referring to what others have said about coming into therapy with their family]: So Miranda, how do you see all of this?

3. Motivational Questions

Try to find out what each person's motivation is for coming to family therapy. In other words, why did they come and what do they hope to get out of the session. It is a well-known observation in all psychotherapy that people need to be motivated to get something out of therapy, or the therapy will not be very successful. That is why court-ordered or other mandated clients are usually the most difficult to treat. Given that this is the case, question 3 of the check-in, which probes for the motivational aspect, is particularly important. If a family member says, "I don't want to be here," or "This wasn't my idea. I was forced by my mom (or dad or spouse) to come here today or else I wouldn't be here," it is important to help them see that there is something for them to gain in coming to the sessions.

This may be accomplished by the therapist responding with, "I know you don't want to be here and wouldn't have come if you felt you had a choice, but now that you are here, is there *anything* in the family that you would like to be different?" This usually brings forth statements such as, "I want to get my mom to stop nagging me." or "I want my parents to leave me alone." or "I want to be relieved of having to be the caretaker for my younger siblings." A "laid back" father may say, "I think my wife is making too big a deal about this problem by dragging all of us into therapy. I'd like her to stop picking on our oldest daughter in particular." These goals can be very instrumental in creating motivation to participate in the therapy.

Here is an example of the therapist checking in with the mother of the family:

> Therapist: Susan, I'm interested to know what you would like to get out of the session today.
>
> Susan: I'm really concerned about the family not spending any time together.
>
> Therapist: I'm interested to know more about what you mean when you say the family doesn't spend any time together...

Other ways of approaching this motivational question include the therapist asking:

- Are there any issues that you would like to discuss today?
- Is there anything that you'd like to see happen today?
- What do you hope to get out of this session today?

In regard to choosing when to use follow-up questions in the check-in, the therapist must strike a balance between two factors. On the one hand, particularly if it is a large family, she cannot spend too much time on any one person since she needs to check in with each one of them for an approximately equal length of time. On the other hand, she needs to draw each member out enough to feel like she has gotten something of substance from each one. At the end of the check-in, the therapist wants to have a picture in her mind of how this person's day looks, of how they are feeling in the moment, and of what it is that they really want from coming to therapy. Is this person cynical about therapy, not able to access his feelings, reluctant to even be in the room? Is another member cooperative, aware of family patterns, psychologically minded?

Finding Allies

Basically, the therapist wants to know the members of the team she is working with, what role they play in the family, and how motivated they are to work things through to a deeper level. It is particularly important to find out who is courageous enough to take risks, and is willing to be honest about themselves and the other family members. This person(s) may become the ally of the therapist, the one(s) whom the therapist can count on to "tell it like it is." The age of these allies can vary from a young seven or eight year old to an older, wise person.

If there are no allies that can be perceived, the therapist may assume that this family is very entrenched in their patterns and there may be too great a level of fear to risk telling their truth. It may be that the family members fear that if they are honest in the session, they will get in trouble afterwards. Such questions can be asked of the family and the way they answer can lead to important understandings for the therapist. In any case, this will probably be a difficult family to work with using this methodology, and the therapist may want to work together with a co-therapist on this case, so she will have someone with whom to collaborate. It is very hard to change a family dynamic without someone else agreeing with the therapist's point of view.

Ten Principles for the Check-In

While the above-mentioned three areas of check-in questioning are fairly concrete, there are also ten fundamental principles that the therapist needs to be concurrently aware of while doing the check-in with the family.

1. Identifying Goals

As people are responding to the check-in questions, it is important for the therapist to notice where interpersonal growth and healing may be needed within the family. The second and third areas of questioning are especially good opportunities for family members to express exactly what they want to get out of the therapy. These responses can inform the therapist as to possible goals to work on in the Direct Interaction phase of the session, which will be discussed more completely later on in the book.

2. Providing Opportunities for Expression

The check-in is a time to help the family feel comfortable and to give each family member an opportunity to express what they want to accomplish in family therapy. During the check-in, it is important that every family member gets his or her turn and that no one is allowed to interrupt him or her during this time. If the session ends up with the major focus on two people, then the less involved people have at least had some time to talk during the check-in and will be less likely to feel left out.

However, it is important to not allow the check-in stage of the session to go on too long. Sometimes one family member will go beyond "checking in," and will begin a lengthy description of something that is very important to him. When this occurs, it is important for the therapist to set a limit by saying, "That sounds very important and we will get back to that. But for now I'd like to make sure everyone gets a chance to check-in." If you do say this, it is important that you get back to that person later in the session or they will find it difficult to build a trusting relationship with you.

3. Follow-Up Questions

As individual family members check-in, they will often make reference to other family members. It can be very helpful to follow up on those references both with the person who made the remark and with the person who was referred to. For example, a wife says, "I really think a big part of the problem is that my husband doesn't have any time for the family." When the therapist is checking in with the husband, it can be helpful for the therapist to say, "What do you think about what your wife has brought up today about your not being involved enough in your family's life?"

Here is an example of how to follow up on what the person who is checking in is saying: An adult daughter says, "My parents divorced ten years ago and I haven't had a relationship with my mom since. There is no way to have a relationship with her." The therapist can follow up on the daughter's statement by saying, "Have you tried to have a relationship with her?" Or, "What's it like to be here with her now?"

4. Equality of Understanding

It is very important that the therapist takes a balanced interest in each family member. The therapist needs to provide equal time, attention, understanding, empathy, and opportunity for each family member to answer the check-in questions. Otherwise, individual family members may feel left out or less important. For example, in a mother-daughter session, if the mother senses that the therapist is showing a lot of interest and understanding for the daughter's position, but is not feeling equally attended to, then it is probable that the mother will feel ignored and may close down emotionally. In short, all family members should feel like the therapist is "on their side."

This is particularly important in families who have a pattern of ganging up on one person. Scapegoating is not helpful in groups or in families, but it is a common phenomenon. In cases where the therapist sees a tendency in this direction, it is crucial that she not join in with the family against that family member, even if she can see how problematic that person is. Rather, the therapist must do her best to show empathy for that person's position and, by doing so, set a model for other family members to do the same. No matter what disturbing behavior or annoying habit someone has, there is usually something in him or her that means well. It is the therapist's job to provide some meaningful context for a behavior that can appear entirely irrational.

5. Building a Safe Container

Building a trusting relationship with *each* family member is a significant prerequisite to doing effective therapy with a family. Each family member needs to feel safe and comfortable in order to do the deep, emotional work that is important for family therapy to be effective. The therapist needs to acknowledge, make contact, and build rapport with each family member. In short, the therapist needs to develop a personal relationship with each individual in the family.

The primary way the therapist goes about creating this trusting environment is through empathy. By using simple questions to try to elicit important information, as well as showing curiosity and interest in each person's story, the therapist tries to create an empathic connection with each person. She needs to attempt to deeply understand each family member. This includes recognizing each person's issues, understanding his or her history and present life, and finding the relationships each one has with other family members. Ultimately, when the therapist is done checking in with a family member, she hopes to have some sense of who that person is and what he has gone through in his life.

6. Impartiality

In certain families there will be one person that some or all of the other family members think is a really difficult person (often the IP). The key to working with this type of situation is being impartial. It is possible that this "difficult" family member has never had the opportunity to express his position to his family members. Or, based on his life experience, it may be a real struggle for him to express his feelings at all. This could be causing or adding to the tension in the family.

It is extremely important to take the time that is needed with this "difficult" person to help him get his story out. Take, for example, a family of three: two teenagers and a mother. The two teens check in first with the therapist and they speak harshly of their mother. When the therapist checks in with the mother, it is important for her to really listen to the mother's point of view and to give her the benefit of the doubt so that she feels acknowledged, understood, and supported. If the children have stated a strong case, it could be easy for the therapist to think, "Gosh, she sounds like she is a really horrible mother." But it is important for the therapist to try to understand what her pain is about. One of the major benefits to withholding judgment about a "difficult" family member is that if she is given adequate time to tell her story, it is possible that the other family members will develop a new understanding of her.

Another important aspect of working with "difficult" family members is looking for and making explicit the missing feeling that is behind what makes the other family members think that one person is strange, rigid, or difficult. It is important that the therapist keep in mind that the "difficult" family member feels something that is influencing the way she acts. She may be experiencing shame, fear, overload, or another difficult feeling that is causing her to act "irrationally." For instance, a mother feels guilty any time she thinks about taking care of her own needs because her parents told her she was selfish when she thought about herself. As a consequence, she may overprotect her kids, which may be very annoying to adult children. It is the therapist's job to help the mother get in touch with and express her feelings in a way that other people can hear. This can further help the other family members to understand why the "difficult" person is acting the way she is.

7. Avoiding Moral Judgments

A therapist's moral judgments can hinder her ability to be empathic with a family member. Regardless of the situation, the important thing is not whether a person meets the therapist's moral standards, but rather that the person feels understood by the therapist. Empathy makes it safe for family members to open up and discuss difficult feelings, which is crucial in order for family members to develop a greater understanding of each other.

A possible scenario is one where the therapist is working with a mother and daughter and the mother is struggling to accept her lesbian daughter's sexuality. It may be tempting for the therapist to want to encourage the mother to become more accepting of her daughter's sexual orientation. However, this would invalidate the mother's feelings, which most likely would lead to her lack of trust in the therapist. Whether or not it seems "politically correct," the mother is in a lot of pain and, if the therapist wants the mother to open up and work through the issues that the mother and daughter have, she needs to feel understood, empathized with, and acknowledged.

If the therapist in any way conveys the attitude of "daughter's right, mother's wrong," then the mother may feel defensive, which would most likely limit her active participation in the session. Getting to the feelings of the situation, not just the facts, is what is relevant. If the mother feels ashamed about her daughter's sexuality, then that is how she feels and it is the therapist's job to elicit and empathize with that feeling.

If the therapist is having difficulty empathizing with a family member, she can try to recall a situation where she was in a similar emotional state as that family member. This may help the therapist to feel the difficult emotions that the person is feeling, as opposed to merely focusing on the content of the situation. In other words, the therapist has to suspend her moral, ethical, and political position, as well as what appears rational, and just try to understand each family member on an emotional level.

Here is an example where the therapist uses empathy and avoids moralizing to help the mother express her difficult feelings about her daughter's sexuality:

Therapist: Can you tell your daughter what it is about her sexuality that is difficult for you?
Mother: I wanted grandchildren. I'm very disappointed.
Therapist (to daughter): Did you know that was a part of it?

Daughter: Yes. I let her down. And now I can't even go home for the holidays.

Mother: I have a problem — it is my youngest daughter. She's too young to understand.

Daughter: I want to let my (younger) sister know about my sexuality.

Mother: She's too young. And I'm not ready for that. It still hurts me a lot.

Therapist: Can you tell your daughter more about why "it hurts"?

Mother: I don't think my friends would approve of my daughter's sexuality.

Therapist: So there would be a lot of shame for you?

Mother: These friends are like family. So I say nothing.

Therapist: That sounds very painful to me. I can't say what to do. But the sad part is that it has broken the two of you up.

Mother: I wanted a different life for her.

Daughter begins to cry.

Therapist: Can you tell your daughter what this is like for you?

Mother: I know that not being able to accept my daughter is my problem, but this situation is very painful for me.

The therapist's empathy can also help the daughter to understand her mother better. It may not completely solve their problems, but it helps them to communicate their feelings and thoughts. That is a major step.

It is important for the therapist not to get over-identified with either position. If she finds herself losing her neutrality and going to bat for either one of them, she needs to stop and ask herself why this issue is so charged for her. This leads to an investigation of the therapist's own counter-transference issues, which are so necessary to work through before working with families.

Perhaps the therapist herself is gay or has friends or family members who had a difficult time "coming out" to their family. It would be tempting to use this situation to "blame" the mom for being so closed-minded and judgmental. This is not in the best interests of either the daughter or the mother. It may temporarily make the daughter feel good that the therapist is validating her position, but ultimately it is the relationship with her mother that is most important to her. Sometimes getting a painful truth out on the table allows for other, more positive, feelings to surface. This is in fact what happened with this mother and daughter. A year later a letter from the daughter to the therapist read as follows: "I feel really honored that the session with my mom got included in the book. It was a pinnacle experience for our relationship and for my development as a queer woman."

In cases where criminal behavior has occurred, the therapist does not have the luxury of avoiding moral judgments. Here, she is required by law to report the behavior to the appropriate authorities. In a family in which it was discovered through some individual sessions with the sixteen-year-old daughter that her father was sexually abusing her, this information had to be filed immediately with Child Protective Services (CPS), in accordance with the Child Abuse and Neglect Reporting Act. Action needed to be taken to insure this girl's safety, which included the removal of the father from the home until he took 100% responsibility for his behavior. The father agreed to go to group therapy, the couple entered marriage counseling, and the therapist continued to see the girl individually. Another family therapist was assigned to see the whole family periodically.

8. Ease the Family into the Session

An important aspect worth pointing out about the three check-in areas of questioning is that they are not usually very emotionally charged. Especially in the first session, it is important to respect that the family may be feeling anxious or uncomfortable about being in therapy or even in the same room together. If the therapist were to begin by asking emotionally charged questions, the family members might feel intimidated, defensive, and possibly averse to continuing therapy.

The therapist wants to learn about the family dynamics, but not at the expense of making the family feel uncomfortable. Thus, it is usually wise to avoid asking the parents about their relationship too early in the therapy. One frequent discovery in family therapy is that the "real" problems in the family go back to the husband and wife, and often back to the grandparents. That is often the **family secret**. The parents may contend that they have only sought out family therapy because of the IP, typically their son or daughter. They see the IP as the problem. Thus, if the therapist asks the parents in the first session, "So how is your relationship?" they may resist the question and respond by saying, "What are you talking about? That's not why we are here."

If the therapist gets a strong sense that the parents are really open-minded about the family problem and eager for insight, then it may feel appropriate to ask about their relationship. But if the parents are really committed to the idea that the problem is the IP, it may be best for the therapist to avoid confronting the parents too quickly. In any case, these questions are more appropriate in the main part of the session rather than as part of the check-in.

9. Working with Resistance

The labeling of a family member or members as an IP can be one of the biggest hindrances to progress in family therapy. One important piece of information the therapist needs to elicit from the check-in questions is which of the family members believe that the problem is due to the IP and which ones realize that the problem is inherent to the family system. Another way to look at this is, "Who in the family is more resistant to change and who in the family is more open to change?" As family members answer the check-in questions, the therapist can assess the situation to see how much resistance there is with each family member. Paying attention to each person's level of resistance helps the therapist in figuring out who will be an "ally" throughout the process of encouraging the family members to look at the bigger picture of their family situation.

Resistance by family members is, of course, on a continuum. One could think of three levels on this scale: At the most resistant level, the family says, "My husband and I decided to bring the family here because Mark (the IP) is getting into a lot of trouble and we're really concerned about him." A less resistant family might say, "My husband and I are here because we are having a disagreement about how to discipline Mark." The least resistant family could say, "My husband and I are having trouble with our marriage. We think the children are being affected, and we want to get help as a whole family." It is rare and delightful to get a family as sophisticated as the one mentioned in the last example.

Many families fall into the "most resistant" category. Their modus operandi is to blame all the family problems on the IP. It is the therapist's job to diffuse the notion of the IP. It is important that the therapist acknowledge that the IP is having some difficulties and that is why the family has come to therapy, but the therapist needs to take it a step further by finding out what else is going on in the family.

The main problem that occurs when family members are overly focused on the IP is that it distracts them from looking at what other dynamics are operating in the family. As the therapist probes to find out what other issues are present in the family, certain family members may object by saying, "I don't know why you want to know about everyone else. The problem is with Heidi." At this point, it is important for the therapist to say, "We will get to Heidi. I know you are concerned about her. But it is important that we find out about other things that are going on in the family." In other words, the therapist is starting to plant seeds that there could be more to the family problems than just what's going on with the IP. It is a way of setting the stage for the possibility of another hypothesis, which is that there is more to the situation than just the IP's problems.

10. Balance of Content and Process

There are two aspects to any communication: the "**what**" and the "**how**." The "what" refers to the content or the facts that are being given. The "how" refers to the way in which the message is delivered. This could be tone of voice, physical gestures, or any non-verbal characteristics accompanying the message being transmitted. When gathering information from family members in the check-in, there will be many facts offered which are crucial to the understanding of the family. However, it is easy to get bogged down in information. It is important to remember that the ways in which the messages are delivered are equally significant for the clinician's attention. Many a family member has proclaimed, "We are just fine," "We all get along well," "My wife and I agree on most everything." The therapist listening to just the facts may be asking herself why this family came into therapy if all is so fine. However, when she listens to and observes more closely the *way* these messages are delivered, she may pick up on the exaggerated attempts to prove the family's health that are characteristic of denial and other defenses. This is the "**how**" which must be looked at along with the "**what**" — the **process** along with the **content.**

Summary

In the initial session, the check-in helps the therapist to get a sense of who each family member is. It is also a step toward building a safe container in which each family member feels trusting enough of the therapist and the process to begin to open up and reveal his or her truth to the other family members. In subsequent sessions, the check-in is utilized more for the purpose of reconnecting with each family member and helping to set the agenda for the session. Check-ins in later sessions are often much richer and more personal than one could expect early on. They provide an opportunity for all the family members to hear what other members are concerned about in their lives at this time, whether or not it has anything to do with the family. This is particularly true with adult families who live in separate domiciles, and may have not even seen each other since the last session.

8.
The Direct Interaction

A crucial aspect of this particular style of family therapy is the focus on creating opportunities for "direct interactions," or two-person encounters, among family members. Direct interactions are excellent opportunities for family members to deeply connect, explore, and heal their relationships with each other. Instead of simply having family members talk to the therapist about their feelings for one another as is done in the check-in, the therapist at this stage tries to facilitate family members talking **directly** to each other. It can be helpful during the check-in for the therapist to be on the lookout for potentially significant interactions that need to take place between different family members.

Suppose two of the members report that they have "unfinished business" with each other, or that there is a high level of emotion between them. This would be an indication that they may be ready for a direct interaction. A direct interaction usually begins after all family members have completed the check-in. The therapist invites one family member to change his seat so that he is sitting next to the member with whom he is to have a direct interaction. The therapist will then invite the family member to say what he had been saying to the therapist directly to the other family member.

For example, the therapist can say, "Shelby, this sounds really important. Can you tell this to your mother directly?" And then, after Shelby has said what she wanted to say, the therapist helps facilitate the communication by saying, "Susan, can you tell Shelby how you feel in response to what she just told you?" The direct interaction continues with help from the therapist to make sure the members are being honest and genuine with one another, rather than attacking or being defensive. Direct interactions are the heart of this approach in that this is where the bulk of the healing takes place. Much of the earlier part of the session is for the purpose of building a safe container for the direct interactions to take place.

Two-person encounters have the advantage of creating maximum intimacy between family members. Having a child speak to both his parents at once can never reach the same depth as when he talks to each of them separately. The aim is to break up the "united front" of the parents and have the child relate authentically with each of his parents, one at a time. The same would be true of a mother speaking to both her children at once. No one can have the exact same feelings for two people and having the two-person encounter makes this more obvious. It would be easy for a parent to say, "I love you both equally," but that is just another myth to be challenged in using this approach. Each dyadic relationship in a family is unique, and nurturing these relationships allows for the most satisfying and intimate contact.

Sometimes a direct interaction can become very explosive. Consider the situation where Jody was encouraged to tell his father, Max, about the feelings of abandonment he experienced in childhood when his dad would go away on long business trips and didn't keep contact. Jody began by raising his voice and saying to his dad, "You were never there for me. You screwed up my life. Now I can never trust anyone again." The therapist intervened as quickly as possible and reminded Jody to use "I" statements rather than "you" statements, and, rather than blaming his father, to tell him what it felt like for him when his dad was gone. When Jody was able to say, "I felt lonely, like you would never come back, and I missed you," this allowed his father to be more empathic rather than defensive. The therapist asked Max how he felt hearing Jody say that, and Max responded authentically by saying, "I'm so sorry. I can understand how you must have felt. I was so confused myself in those days."

Generally speaking, when someone is angry, there are hurt feelings underneath. It is the therapist's job to get each family member to experience and express his most vulnerable feelings so that a deep emotional connection can be made.

How to Choose a Direct Interaction

Since there can be a number of people present in a family therapy session and time is limited, it is important that the therapist carefully choose which family members would be the best candidates to have a direct interaction. By listening carefully during the check-in of various members, the therapist should get a good sense of who in the family may be ready to talk directly to a family member and who is emotionally available to receive a direct interaction.

Generally speaking, a direct interaction should be focused on working through obstacles in an interpersonal relationship. In other words, the therapist is seeking out the problem areas in the family and facilitating the healing of those areas through two-person direct encounters. Let us begin with what would *not* be a good choice for a direct interaction. If a daughter checks in about a positive development between herself and her mother, that is not something that the therapist would necessarily choose for a direct interaction. It would be important to acknowledge the positive gains by saying, "What has that been like to connect with your mom more?" And then when checking in with the mother, it is helpful to get her feedback on how she sees the recent connection with her daughter. The direct interactions are better saved for more problematic issues.

Another situation to avoid making into a direct interaction would be if a family member seems flippant in making jokes about other people or exaggeratedly blaming the IP for all the family's problems. If this person doesn't seem open to heartfelt communication, it would be unlikely for a deep connection to occur, and, therefore, the time would not be used well. It may be better to approach the resistant or difficult person by saying, "It seems a little hard for you to be here today. Is that accurate?" Often, by giving this person some undivided attention, he will settle down and become more authentic.

Similarly, if two people seem very angry at each other, it may be best not to start off with a direct interaction between them. Rather, as they see others relating in more vulnerable ways to each other, this may soften them and get them ready for a more authentic connection later on in the session or in a future session.

Essentially, the therapist should look for **emotional readiness** to determine which family members are ready for a direct interaction. For example, one family member may become teary during the check-in. Or, another family member may start to talk with another person during the check-in and the therapist has to hold the interaction off so that all members could check in. Another possibility is that one family member mentions feeling distant or disconnected from another family member. All of these are examples of leads to potentially fruitful direct interactions. Ultimately, the family member that has the most obvious concern involving another member is the best candidate for a direct interaction. If the therapist is aware of two potential encounters, it may be best to begin with the less heated one as a warm-up to the more significant one.

What follows is an example from a check-in with an adult son (James) talking about his relationship with his father (Joseph) as an example of some of these principles:

James: I guess I'd like to feel more connected to my family.

Therapist: Does anyone in particular come to mind?

James: I think my relationship with my dad needs some work.

Therapist: So that would be a goal?

James: Yes.

Therapist: Is there an obstacle there?

James: No, we just didn't do much bonding.

Therapist: Why, was he working a lot?

James: Yeah. He was busy.

Therapist: How has this lack of bonding affected your life?

James: It made it difficult for me to trust.

Therapist: So, a difficulty trusting. (Pause) This is an important issue. We're going to go around and hear everyone's goals for the session and then we'll get back to this.

Since the family was still in the check-in phase, the therapist mentally noted that the father-son interaction was an important one and considered this as having a good potential for a direct interaction. Once all members had completed the check-in, the therapist returned to the father and son. She asked the father to switch seats with another family member so the two were sitting next to each other. They were then asked to physically turn their chairs towards each other so they were directly facing each other. Here is how this interaction got started:

Therapist (to father): Joseph, I want to set the stage for you and James to talk about your difficulty bonding. You can start with what it is like to sit across from each other.

Joseph: I'm comfortable.

Therapist (to son): And how about you?

James: It is intense. We have work to do. I have lots of feelings. I feel overwhelmed.

Therapist: Well let's start with that, "I feel overwhelmed." Can you say that to your dad?

James: Well, I could start with my needs.

Therapist: No, I think it would be good to start with how you feel.

Keeping the Interaction Focused

When two family members sit facing each other directly during a direct interaction, it can be a scary and intense moment. It is not uncommon for family members to have stored up a lot of difficult feelings about each other and to have avoided talking about these feelings for years or decades. Naturally, people in this situation may feel very uncomfortable and may try to manage their anxiety by changing the subject, rationalizing what went wrong in the relationship, providing a quick solution to the problem, intellectualizing, or outright blaming of the other person. It is important for the therapist to realize this and do her best to keep the interaction focused and heartfelt. The therapist does this by encouraging the family member to speak from his heart and express the deep feelings that he has been withholding from this particular family member.

As part of keeping family members on track, the therapist needs to avoid forcing her own agenda on the family. She does not need to try to figure out the solution to the family member's issues and tell him how to fix them. Ideally, in the direct interaction, the therapist's focus is on setting the stage for the family members, making minimal interventions, and allowing the family members to do their own work. The interventions that the therapist does make are informed by whatever is unfolding in the present moment between the two family members. The therapist can watch for cues as to what is the most important thing that seems to be emerging between these two people and then help them to deepen those issues.

One way to pick up on important cues is to watch for **strong feelings** in the form of eyes tearing up, shaking of the voice or the hands, sometimes accompanied by words such as "I'm scared," "I'm angry," or "I feel overwhelmed." When these feelings arise, the therapist can highlight them. In the above example the son said, "I feel overwhelmed." The therapist highlighted this strong feeling by saying, "Well, let's start with that: 'I feel overwhelmed.'" The son then suggested talking about his needs first. The therapist gently kept the interaction focused by encouraging him to focus on and express how he feels in the moment, leaving him to explore what he needs from his dad for later in the session. The son was very clear that he felt overwhelmed and since that is a very strong feeling, the therapist thought it was best to encourage him to develop that emotion.

Building on the above example, let us look at how the therapist keeps the two family members on track while working with strong feelings.

James (son): I missed not having you in my life more.

Joseph (father): There's lots of time left [in our lives].

Therapist: I know it is tempting to solve the problem but it may be best to just listen to him.

This is another example of how the therapist encouraged a family member to stay with how they are feeling in the moment and not get distracted by such things as "solving the problem."

Joseph (father): I was isolated during my childhood.

Therapist (to James): Did you know that?

Joseph: No, I never told him that.

James: Dad, I didn't know that. That explains a lot. It sounds very difficult.

Therapist (to James): It is easy to switch into the role of caretaker to your dad. But it is important for you to speak about how you feel.

The above is another instance of how the therapist encourages the family members to stay with their feelings and express them directly to the person with whom they are speaking. The son's attempt to take care of the father was a nice gesture, but ultimately a distraction to the goal of having father and son express how they feel about each other, which is where the healing takes place. The therapist is looking for the factors that prevented these two people from having a closer relationship. In this case, the father and son didn't spend much time together and failed to bond in a deep way. Thus, it is important to get to their feelings about what it was like not to have had this connection. This will help them to develop empathy and avoid mutual blaming. Then they are ready to explore what they want from each other *now* in their relationship.

Closing a Direct Interaction

After two people engage in an important piece of work, as this father-son interaction displayed, it may seem like a good time to close the direct interaction. The therapist should not cut the two family members short, but if what needed to emerge has been completed, then it is a good opportunity to end the interaction and move on. A direct interaction usually has a beginning, middle, and end. The therapist will often feel when the interaction is complete. For example, the flow of conversation stops, there is a pause, or the people may spontaneously hug one another. There is a feeling in the room that this conversation is done for now. Let us see how the above example was concluded:

James: Nothing can replace the contact.

Joseph: It is true. I regret it.

Therapist (to James): What's that feel like to hear that?

James: It really touches me.

Therapist (after a long pause): Is this an okay time to stop for now?

This became a natural stopping point for this direct interaction. When the therapist asks, "Is this a good place to stop for the moment?", the son may say, "I want to just say one more thing to my dad." Of course he is encouraged to do so. Or he may say, "Yes, that feels complete." If these are the only two family members present in the session, the therapist may want to encourage them to continue talking. However, when there are three or more family members present, it is important that the therapist consider getting the other family members involved. There will always be time later in the session or during another session for the two family members who had the direct interaction to further discuss their relationship.

Handling Direct Interactions When Problems Are Not Being Solved

For example, what if the two people involved are still angry and defensive, and no movement seems to be occurring? One possibility is to shift to another related direct interaction that may have more mileage. Let us look at the example of Denise, an adult child with her sister and parents in a family session. Denise and her mother were engaged in an intense interaction about a night twelve years ago when Denise was sixteen. Her mom, frustrated by Denise's lowered grades in school and generally uncommunicative behavior, came into her room and started shaking her, saying, "What's wrong with you?" In the heat of this interaction, Denise shouted out that she had been raped four years ago and hadn't told anyone about it. Mother's response to Denise was, "You see, you always wanted to grow up too fast." She was implying that because Denise had always hung out with older boys, she had it coming to her and deserved what she had gotten. Denise felt that her mother had no compassion for her in that interaction twelve years ago and walled herself off from her mom ever since.

In the midst of this direct interaction with her mom, in which mom was continuing to defend herself, Denise flashed on this memory of her dad being outside the room when she and her mother were fighting. This image allowed Denise to get in touch with the angry feelings she had about her dad for not protecting her. As this happened, the therapist suggested that she switch seats so that she could now have a direct interaction with her father.

In this interaction, Denise was able to tell her dad what she felt like when he failed to come to her aid in any way during this incident. It emerged through this interaction that her father had felt guilty ever since then and had withdrawn from his relationship with his daughter because of the shame associated with that. He was now able to relay this to Denise and she was moved to hear it.

The therapist then wondered aloud if the father had felt torn between his wife and his daughter. The father acknowledged that he had wanted to protect his daughter but was afraid to confront his wife whom he found intimidating. It then became fertile ground for the parents to have a direct interaction. Eventually, Denise and her mother resumed their direct interaction, but now both were in a very different emotional state from which to speak and to listen. As the mother had witnessed both Denise and her husband expressing their vulnerability, she saw that she was not being singled out as the one to blame and became more interested in repairing the damage done in her relationship with her daughter.

Getting Feedback

In the example above of Denise's family, no direct requests for feedback were needed since the movement from one direct interaction to the next occurred organically. However, this is not always the case. Sometimes, it is necessary for the therapist to check in with other family members once a direct interaction is completed. This gets other family members more involved in the session and it can transition into another direct interaction. To encourage feedback after the close of a direct interaction, the therapist can ask the observing family members, "How did each of you feel during that interaction?" Or, "Did anybody have a reaction to that?" Or, "What was that like for all of you to observe that?" For example, if one sibling has a direct encounter with a parent, it may stir up a lot of emotion for the other sibling(s), who may now choose to have an interaction with the parent as well. When there are only two people in the session, such as a mother and daughter, the therapist can ask them how it was to have that interaction, thus getting them to step back from the encounter and observe the process.

Starting a New Direct Interaction

Once one direct interaction comes to a close and feedback is given, the next step is to encourage another direct interaction. Based on the feedback that was offered, it may be clear that one person was triggered by the interaction they observed. A daughter may say with tears in her eyes, "Seeing my brother and father connected like that made me feel left out. I feel really sad now." That kind of reply gives the therapist the option of replying, "Why don't you switch seats and sit across from your father and let him know how you're feeling?"

Timing of Direct Interactions

The success of the direct interaction is based on the safety that is established in the therapy room. It is often the case that the family is not ready to participate in direct interactions because they are too angry with one another, they have not met for a while and feel distant from one another, or they do not feel trusting enough of themselves, each other, or of the therapist to take a risk of this nature. There is no point in pushing for this to happen when the safe container has not yet developed.

The Haskell family initially began therapy when the father was dying of a terminal illness. The three adult sons and their mother sought treatment so that they could work on their issues with the father before he died. Sessions began in the family home since the dad was not physically able to leave the house. After the father died, the remaining family members felt they wanted to continue working together dealing with their grief around the father's death. After about a year, when the major issues had been dealt with, the family felt they wanted to continue therapy once a month since each of the family members felt trust in the therapist and in the safety of the consulting room. Sessions were regularly two hours long and were scheduled once a month. Since they all had their own separate lives and didn't live together, the family members did not feel ready to dive into direct interactions when they first walked in the door. Thus, the first hour of these sessions was spent with prolonged check-ins, where each member enjoyed the space to discuss what was going on in their lives that was most meaningful to them right now. They would also include whether they had anything they wanted to "work on" during that session with any member(s) of the family.

The second hour was spent doing direct interactions. Because the therapist had worked with the father (husband) and had been with the family through their grieving process, the therapy room became the sacred container for other difficult interactions to occur. After the initial hour of the check-in, the family members felt safe enough to dip into their own vulnerability and take the risk of directly encountering one another. This is one reason that having two-hour family sessions tends to be most beneficial.

Deepening the Direct Interaction

When two family members are engaged in a direct interaction, there are certain interventions the therapist can make to help deepen the communication. As mentioned above, a direct interaction between two family members can be intense and anxiety-provoking. It is likely that the family members will need help in communicating directly and clearly with each other. The therapist's goal is to allow the family members to do as much work as they can on their own, but to give help when it is needed. Any intervention that is made should be as simple as possible so it does not throw the family members off track or obstruct the natural flow. Below is a list of some of the helpful interventions a therapist can make during a direct interaction:

1. If a family member is feeling overwhelmed emotionally, help them to slow down and stay present with the moment.

It can sometimes be very difficult for family members to speak directly to each other about how they feel. If during a direct interaction, a family member looks like they are in shock or they are struggling to speak or they are getting angry, it can be helpful to slow the process down and work with them around what feelings are present for them in that moment.

For example, the therapist may say, "I notice you're getting angry. What are you feeling now?" Or "Let's stay with that. What's going on?" It may take only a moment to settle the person down. The other benefit is that important hidden feelings may surface during those moments if the person is given the chance to access them. In essence, the therapist is the guardian of the conversation.

April had waited a long time to get her family into therapy. Her brother and father flew across the country for the occasion and April was very nervous about how the session would go. She was very angry with her older brother and felt that he had always been condescending to her and didn't recognize her for her intelligence, perceptiveness, and worthiness as a person. When she began to talk to him in a direct interaction, she became tongue-tied and confused about what she wanted to say. She didn't know where to start. It seemed that just the presence of her brother was eliciting the same feelings that she had often felt with him in the past.

The therapist could see the struggle April was having and encouraged her to slow down and take a few breaths. She empathized with her nervousness and validated that, of course, it would be difficult to be so up front with her brother when she had always felt intimidated in interactions with him. Seeing that she had an ally in the therapist and feeling more centered through her breathing, April was able to garner her confidence and went on to talk more directly to her brother. Instead of being confused, she was able to say to him, "I have always felt scared of you and felt that you were judging me."

2. Pay attention to body language and non-verbal gestures.

During a direct interaction, a family member may get very emotional or express something with his body. It is important to observe these cues. For example, if Sunny starts getting teary as she says, "My mom and I used to be best friends," then it is clear that her perception that they are no longer best friends is very painful for her. A good follow-up question could be, "Can you tell your mom how important she is to you?"

Pointing out incongruity between verbal and non-verbal behavior can also be helpful. For instance, a daughter acknowledges a difficulty in expressing anger, smiles as she tells her mom how angry she is for having been her caretaker all these years. A therapist could point this out by saying, "I hear you saying that you are angry with your mom and yet I see you smiling as you are talking to her." This challenging of the "smiling defense," may allow the daughter to then cry over how much she has had to suppress her real feelings.

3. Ask simple questions to try to better understand what someone is saying.

For example, Adam, a son, says, "I have a lot of trouble talking to my mother." The therapist can ask, "What is the problem?" Adam: "I feel like I dissociate when I talk to her." Therapist: "What is that like?"

4. Clarify and summarize what a family member is saying to make sure that the receiving member understands what message the sending member is giving.

For example, Teresa talks for a while about being upset with her mother for allowing her emotionally abusive father to take custody of her. The therapist can say, "I guess what you're saying to your mom is 'how could you leave me with him?'"

5. Encourage family members to move their chairs if need be and speak directly to each other.

Anytime two people have a direct interaction they should sit next to each other and then move their chairs so they are facing each other directly. The therapist can say, "Why don't you two switch chairs so you can speak directly with each other?" If the family member says, "No, I don't feel like getting any closer to this person right now," this should be respected and they can speak from where they are. This often occurs in cases where abuse of various kinds has occurred and the "victim" of the abuse doesn't feel comfortable moving into the "energy field" of the perpetrator. In these cases, whatever communication they are able to have is usually better than not speaking at all.

6. Encourage straight talk.

This has to do with supporting family members to speak their truths, as opposed to taking care of other people or holding back feelings due to fear. For example, Martha, a mother who tended to blame herself for the actions of her children said to her son Bryan, "I know I haven't been the easiest person to live with, but..." Seeing her voice get lower as her hands begin fidgeting, the therapist said, "Why don't you let Bryan know what's on your mind?"

7. Encourage family members to use "I" statements and lead with their own feelings, as opposed to blaming other people.

If family members blame each other, they will not make much progress in terms of having a heartfelt communication. Attacking typically breeds defensiveness. Family members may need a lot of encouragement to speak about their true feelings since doing so can make them feel very vulnerable.

For example, Jennifer is talking to her father, Henry, about his never following through with their relationship once he got remarried to another woman and had children with her. She is telling dad, "You never really cared about me. You always put your other children first." The therapist predicts that such statements will make dad defensive and suggests to Jennifer that she speak about herself instead. The therapist asks her, "How did that feel to you when your dad seemed to pay more attention to the other children?" Jennifer responds with, "I guess I felt invisible or unimportant." The therapist then encourages her to tell that directly to her father.

8. Remind people to communicate with each other in specific and concrete terms.

Sweeping generalizations such as "always" or "never" or labeling someone as "scary" or "mean" are not as effective as letting them know about specific examples of their behavior.

The therapist says to Elizabeth who is feeling intimidated by her son, Tom, "Do you want to tell him specific behaviors he has that intimidate you?"

9. Try to understand each family member's inner experience.

For example, a mother might say, "I didn't realize I was that important to her (the daughter)." The therapist can reply by asking the daughter, "How does it feel to hear that?" Or to continue with the example of Elizabeth and Tom about his intimidating behaviors, the therapist questions mom, "What happens inside of you when he does this?"

10. As interactions get more heated, remind each person to continue to speak directly to the family member being addressed.

As the interaction gets more intense, people can easily forget to speak directly to each other. The therapist needs to encourage people to "stay with each other" while communicating. For example, the mother begins talking to the therapist instead of to her son. The therapist encourages mom by saying, "Stay with him," while gesturing the mom back to her son.

11. If one family member starts to overwhelm the other member with too many issues or details, stop them and get a response from the other family member.

One family member may get on a roll and express many issues one after another. As a result, the receiving family member may feel overwhelmed and have difficulty replying to anything that was said. The therapist can simply stop the son who is speaking and say, for example, "You've said a lot. Let's give your mom a chance to respond."

12. Family members that are on the listening end of an interaction may need to be prompted to reply to something that was said to them, especially if it contains strong emotional content.

For example, Michael expresses to his mom that he would like her to show more interest in him, to ask about his life more, and mom isn't saying anything. The therapist may need to prompt a response from mother by saying, "It sounds like Michael wants to have a better connection with you. What would that be like for you?"

Or another example is Jameka, a biracial daughter, telling her mother that she feels her mother was less interested in her because her mother is white. The therapist can check this out with the mother non-judgmentally by saying, "So, is there anything to that?"

13. Carefully confront family members when necessary.

Confronting a family member has to be done very carefully. Sometimes offering a client your insights or your wisdom may not be well received, even if you try to do it with compassion. If the family member feels judged in any way, he or she will usually shut down emotionally. But compassion alone may not be enough either. Letting people know that you understand them and realize how hard their situation is may not be enough to provide the push for them to grow. Thus, there is a blend of compassion and confrontation that is useful to have, which gets easier to do with practice.

In one divorced family, Lance, an adult son whose dad had left the family by the time Lance was a year old, was sharing with his dad the feeling that when he went on supervised visits with him at age 4 or 5, he remembered coming home and feeling put down and consequently bad about himself. Lance's father, Harry, kept defending himself, assuring Lance that he always treated Lance and his brother Mel the same way, and that he and Mel had a fine relationship. It seemed that no matter what Lance said to his dad in the session, dad was impervious to Lance's feelings. At that point, the therapist took a firmer stand and said to the father, "Harry, I know you are convinced that you did nothing to make Lance feel bad about himself, but the fact is, he felt that way. Judging from the emotion that Lance is expressing, it seems that something must have happened in those visits that was harmful to him."

The therapist still felt like she was up against a wall in talking to Harry until she remembered that Sarah, Lance's mom, had said earlier in the session that Lance was her favorite child and she always babied him. The therapist wondered aloud whether Harry might have been less loving to Lance because of his anger at his ex-wife whom he now associated with Lance. At this point in the session, Lance revealed that his mom used to tell him mostly negative things about his dad, including that he was often delinquent in paying child support. Hearing all this allowed Harry to reevaluate the situation somewhat since he saw that both his and Lance's negative feelings towards each other were influenced by Lance's relationship with his mom. Now Harry and Sarah began to face their own issues, allowing Lance to have a cleaner relationship with his dad. Thus, confronting Harry was not enough in itself. It was only when the surface area of the problem was expanded to include Sarah that Harry could be more flexible in understanding his relationship with Lance.

14. Encourage family members to stay present to the immediate situation.

Sometimes a family member, like George, will say to his wife, Sally, "That's exactly what my mother does to me." That may be important, but it pulls the direct interaction out of the present. It is important for the therapist to say, "Let's not switch to your mother right now. Stay with Sally."

The mom who blames herself for her children's problems says to the therapist as a reason for why she is intimidated by her son, "My father was very intimidating." The therapist responds with, "Well, let's not put it all on your father. Stay with your son. Let him know how you feel."

15. Summarize both family members' points of view to make sure that each person understands the other person.

This is similar to point #4 above, where the goal is to clarify and summarize what one person has said to another. However, when two family members are intensely engaged, the therapist can try to summarize the main points of both people simultaneously. The therapist says to the mother, Elizabeth, "So I guess what you are saying to Tom is, 'I get intimidated by you.' And I guess, Tom, what you are saying to your mom is, 'I don't like it when you try to control what I do.'"

16. Identify typical family patterns, such as caretaking for another person instead of expressing one's own needs.

Families may exhibit certain patterns such as abandonment, mistrust, competition, lack of vulnerability, or caretaking. It can be helpful for the therapist to point these patterns out to the family. Elizabeth, the mother in the above example says to her son Tom, "It is like you get so angry. I'm worried that you'll lose your friends if you treat them like this." The therapist interrupts mom by saying, "It is easy to switch into the role of caretaker...to try to make sure Tom is getting along with other people okay. There seems to be a lot of that going on in this family. But it is important for you, Elizabeth, to speak about how *you* feel. What about *your* needs?"

Let us look at an example of some of these interventions in action. The interventions listed above correspond to the order that they appear in the example below and are noted in parentheses with the intervention number. We continue with the mom and son, Elizabeth and Tom.

> Therapist: Elizabeth, what was that like to observe your husband and son discussing their relationship?
>
> Elizabeth: Well it was, uh, I guess good. (Pause) I mean I don't know. I'm feeling really confused.
>
> Therapist: Let's stay with that. What's going on? (1)
>
> Elizabeth: I just feel torn.

Therapist: Well just stay with that torn feeling for a moment. (Pause) I notice you're slumping your head. Is there some sadness there? (1, 2)

Elizabeth: Well, yes. I mean I'm glad to see Paul and his dad connecting. But I guess I am a little sad about my relationship with Tom (her other son).

Therapist: What is it that is upsetting you? (3)

Elizabeth: I just don't feel like we can talk anymore.

Therapist: It sounds like you're feeling disconnected from your son. Well why don't you two switch chairs so you can talk directly to each other. (4, 5)

Therapist: Why don't you let Tom know what's on your mind? (6)

Elizabeth: You try to intimidate me, Tom.

Therapist: See if you can lead with your feelings. I feel... (7)

Elizabeth (to Tom): Well, I feel intimidated by you whenever I do something that you don't like.

Therapist: Do you want to tell him specific behaviors that he does that intimidate you? (8)

Elizabeth: He gets agitated, talks loudly, with lots of feeling...

Therapist: What happens inside of you when he does this? (9)

Elizabeth: I feel small. I get overwhelmed. (Elizabeth looks at therapist and away from Tom.)

Therapist: Stay with him (i.e., talk directly to him). (10)

Elizabeth: It is hard for me to communicate with him...hard for me to speak my truth.

Therapist: You've said a lot Elizabeth. Let's give Tom a chance to respond. (Turning toward Tom): Do you know what she's talking about? (11)

Tom: Yes.

Therapist: Do you have anything to say about it? (12)

Tom answers to therapist.

Therapist: Talk to your mom directly. (10)

Tom: (he faces his mom and continues) I'm sorry. That's just who I am.

Therapist: So is that the way it is going to be? You'll continue as the intimidator? (13)

Therapist (to Elizabeth): How does that make you feel?

Elizabeth: My father was very intimidating.

Therapist: Well, let's not put it all on your father. Stay with Tom. Let him know how you feel. (14)

Elizabeth: Tom, I really struggle to communicate with you when I feel intimidated.

Therapist: What does that bring up for you, Tom? (12)

Tom: I get really frustrated at the way you always try to tell me what to do.

Therapist: So I guess what you're saying to Tom is, "I get intimidated by you." And I guess what you're saying to your mom is, "I don't like it when you try to control what I do." (15)

Elizabeth: It is like you get so angry. I'm worried that you'll lose your friends if you treat them like this.

Therapist: It is easy to switch into the role of caretaker... to try to make sure Tom is getting along with other people okay. There seems to be a lot of that going on in this family. But it is important for you to speak about how you feel. What about your needs? (16)

Working with Subsystems

Sometimes it makes sense to work with a subsystem of the group. For example, if it becomes apparent that the family problem is focused on the couple and the children are less involved, then it may be time for the therapist to suggest giving the children a break and working with the couple separately. But this is a judgment call, because, even if the problem is essentially with the parents or grandparents, the children can be a big asset in the session.

Suppose the husband is very domineering and the wife doesn't stand up for herself. If the husband constantly blames the wife and she consistently takes responsibility for all the problems, then it can be difficult for the therapist to stimulate change. However, if the children are present, one of them may say, "Dad is always intimidating everyone, including mom. And she can't stand up for herself." This is information that the therapist may not have gotten so directly if the children were not present at the session. Hearing this from the children may then make it easier for the therapist to confront the parents about their roles in the family system.

Concrete Changes

It is not necessary that every session get tied up neatly at the end. Confusion can stimulate a lot of growth for the family. But sometimes, as a session comes to a close, it is appropriate to discuss concrete changes that family members can make. This is especially true for a family that won't be meeting for a while. Often, in these cases, delving too deeply into the past may not be the best plan of action. The focus may be on present, concrete changes that can be made. For example, let's look at how the session from the example above came to a close:

> Therapist: I see we are running out of time. I know we won't have a chance to meet for another month and I realize that the two of you are really struggling to communicate better. Can the two of you make some type of agreement about this controlling-intimidating issue?
>
> Elizabeth: I'm going to think about what you said about me being controlling. I realize that could be frustrating for you. In fact, if you notice me doing that, I would encourage you to let me know in a respectful way. That could really help.
>
> Therapist: How does it feel to hear that, Tom?
>
> Tom: It sounds good. I will let you know.
>
> Therapist: And how about you, Tom? Are you interested in feedback around being intimidating? Is that something you would like to change?
>
> Tom: Um, yeah. I think if she were to stop trying to control me, I would be able to cut out the intimidating part.

9.
Check-Out

It is very important to do a check-out before closing any family therapy session. If there are more than two people in the room, it is possible that some of those people may not have had an opportunity to speak since the check-in. The purpose of the check-out is to find out how the session went for each person and to bring some closure to the meeting. The therapist can say, "I see we are running out of time. Why don't we find out how this session has been for each of you?"

After completing the go-round, the therapist can add, "Is there anything else anybody wants to say to another family member or to me?" Family members will often say some really nice things to each other at the end of a session. After a very intense session between Hera and her mom, where Hera had told her mom some of the ways her childhood had been very painful, the two were asked if there was anything else they wanted to add. Hera took her mom's hands and said, "I love you." Her mom responded in kind and the two of them hugged in a very loving way.

The check-out is also a good time to find out who in the family is interested in continuing the therapy and who is more reluctant. This is good information to have in predicting what may happen in future sessions.

Therapist Note-Taking

While some therapists may feel more comfortable taking notes during a session, it is far more effective in this kind of experiential family therapy to be as fully present as possible during the sessions. Thus, it is best not to take notes during sessions. However, it is also very important to remember as much as one can about the main themes of the last session, to be able to juxtapose that with the new issues that the family brings up in the current session. Therefore, detailed note taking after the session is the preferred way to provide a bridge for the family to the next session.

It is beneficial to write down not only the major themes that occurred during the session, but also as many details as possible, particularly about the direct interactions. It is good to note who in the family got to speak the most, as well as the least, who may have felt left out, who got into their feelings in a deep way, and what was left unfinished. Keeping all of this in mind and having it available through reading the notes before the session, not only allows the therapist to maintain a balance among the members in terms of participation, but also helps the family feel the strength of the container provided by the therapist. In fact, the family members may not always remember what happened at the last session, so it is reassuring for them to know that the therapist has a good sense of this and, therefore, continuity is preserved.

Subsequent Sessions

As stated earlier, it is important to start every session with a check-in. Whether the family attends weekly, bi-weekly, or monthly sessions, the therapist can say, "Let's start with a check-in," or "How is it going today?" or "What specifically do you each want to work on today? Who wants to start?" Typically, the therapist should lean towards a question that asks each family member what his or her goal is for the session. If your question is, "How has your past week (month) been?" people may fall into intellectual reporting about the past, which would not be as productive.

During check-ins, the therapist should look for two things. First, she wants to keep in mind the initial presenting problem that the family came into therapy with and compare that to what the family brings in subsequently. The original presenting problem is the baseline. If the therapist knows what the baseline is, then she can be a better judge of how far the family has progressed.

Secondly, she needs to pay attention to the changes in relationships among the family members. Relationships are the therapist's lifeline. She wants to know whom each person connected with outside of the session and what the quality and quantity of the interaction was. For example, a daughter may check in by saying she is feeling closer to her parents now and is seeing them once a week. A son may report that he still feels isolated from the family and has been having little interaction with any of the members. Both of these reports give the therapist an idea of what is happening now within the family and what may need to be further explored in the session.

Termination

While termination is a big part of the process in individual therapy, in CFFT it is less of a focus. The idea of termination usually comes from the family themselves rather than from the therapist. Once it is brought up in a session, the therapist can begin to discuss with the family whether their goals for treatment have been met, and what would be the advantages and disadvantages of continuing further. Each member should be encouraged to talk about how things have changed for him in the family, how the family as a whole has changed, and what his preferences are about whether or not to end therapy.

It is a good idea to have several sessions after the initial mention of termination by the family, to review what has transpired in the course of therapy. This also serves to make sure that the initial idea of ending still seems like a good one a few weeks later, and for the family and therapist to bring some closure to their relationship. The therapist is generally supportive of the family going on its own but reminds them that they can also come back to see her in the future. In this sense, the family therapist is more like the family doctor than an individual therapist would be. It often happens that a part of a family, such as the couple, may choose to return at a later time.

Especially when the family has been coming to therapy for six months or longer, it is likely that strong bonds have developed between the therapist and the family members. In keeping with the notion of authenticity that is a core of this approach, the therapist can feel free to express her honest feelings of loss to the family if this feels appropriate. When the therapist and family say good-bye to each other, they are usually wishing each other well and letting each other know they care. They are acknowledging to one another that they have shared a deep experience together and that they will carry each other with them in their hearts and in their minds.

10.
Common Mistakes Made by Family Therapists

Practicing family therapy can sometimes feel like walking on a tightrope in that the therapist is doing her best to keep things balanced. Thus, she wants to encourage members to look at difficult material without scaring them out of the room. She wants to give new ideas to the family while still showing respect and concern for the way they have been seeing the problem. She wants to give everyone a turn to speak without alienating the people who are trying to interrupt. Choosing to enter family therapy is one of the scariest decisions a family can make and the therapist must be aware of that fear at every moment without letting it interfere with the work that needs to be done. In this chapter we will look at some of the potential problems therapists must avoid in their practice.

Focusing on the IP

Given that learning family therapy requires learning a whole new paradigm, it is easy to see how mistakes can be made. For one, if the therapist buys into the notion that the family is there for the IP and there are no other problems in the family except the IP, this could be very damaging to the IP. Now, in addition to his parents blaming everything on him, he has an outside authority doing the same thing. This can only deepen his guilt and sense of low self-esteem, and will not help in resolving the family's problem.

Lynn was taken to a therapist by her abusive single mother when she was fifteen years old. Mother and daughter were in an enmeshed relationship, and the mother brought the daughter into a local family therapy clinic. Mother convinced the relatively young family therapist that Lynn was the problem and Lynn was referred for individual treatment. The abuse continued at home for years until Lynn finally moved out of the state, but not without major psychological problems to be healed.

Not Focusing on the IP

On the other hand, it can be a big mistake to insist to the parents that it is *not* the IP who has the problem. Pointing to the relationship between the parents or difficulties that other siblings seem to be having may anger the parents and prevent them from returning to therapy. The parents' real concern about the IP must be taken seriously. They must feel heard and not dismissed as resistant, stubborn, or uncooperative.

In a way, doing family therapy is like walking a tightrope. One does not want to err on either side because this will not help the family.

Counter-Transference

When there are so many different sides of a story being told, it is easy for a new family therapist to believe some people in the family more than others. Especially if the therapist has unresolved feelings with her own family members, it is easy to place "blame" and "innocence" onto family members without sufficient evidence.

The Wolff family came into treatment because of a problem the older daughter, Lois, was having at school. Her teachers had claimed that Lois skipped school, hung out with a tough crowd, and seemed to be going down a destructive path. Dr. Wolff, a physician of some stature, had strong opinions about why Lois was having these symptoms. He believed it was because her mother did not set proper boundaries on her behavior and "let her get away with murder." Dr. Wolff said that his wife consistently undermined him in his efforts to set his daughter straight. Mrs. Wolff presented as more of a free spirit, disparaging of the teacher's report and of her husband's concerns. It was easy for this young therapist to take sides with the father, especially since she had come from a family in which her father was a physician, too, and she had a great deal of respect for him. Although the therapist tried hard to listen to each person's narrative, she unintentionally cut the mom off several times until Mrs. Wolff got very angry with her, and managed to pull the whole family out of treatment.

Allowing Interruptions

Another common error occurs when the therapist allows people to interrupt each other during the check-in. If the therapist doesn't set the ground rules that no one is allowed to interrupt when someone else is doing a check-in, then the chaos that results can cause a sense of hopelessness in the family. Members may get the sense that people will speak over each other just like they do at home and that the therapist is not strong enough to set boundaries and create a safe container.

Letting One Member Speak for Too Long

Related to allowing interruptions is another mistake that occurs when the therapist lets a member go on too long in the check-in, listing a series of complaints about a particular family member, often the IP. It can be very painful for an individual to have to sit and listen to a detailed account of what people find objectionable about his behavior and not be able to defend himself. Although beginning therapists may find it difficult to "cut people off" when they clearly want to go on talking, this is a skill that must be developed if one is to work with families. A therapist could say in a friendly way, "I know you have a lot that you want to say, Mrs. Harner, but it is important for us to hear a check-in from each of the family members first before we get into such detail." This saves the IP or other family member from being totally humiliated and lets the mother know that the therapist, not she, is in control of the session.

Error of Exclusion

The error of exclusion is a frequent one as well. Just as in any group, there is a tendency for the most verbal or the loudest people to get the most airtime. It is the therapist's job to see that all the members get a chance to speak if they choose to. Someone might interrupt and be cut off by the therapist, but then, later on, it is important for the therapist to go back to that person and inquire about what they wanted to say. If the therapist forgets to go back to the family member, the member can begin to feel mistrustful of the therapist.

Sometimes a particular dyad such as dad and son can take the spotlight for a while. This is fine given that productive work is being done between them. The error would be to end the session there, without asking the other members for feedback on this direct interaction, and neglecting to do a check-out with all the family members.

Sometimes the parents will get into an argument in the session and the therapist gets so wrapped up in their material that she forgets to check in with the children. This can result in the children feeling invisible and unnecessary, which would make them less likely to want to return. Of course, sometimes this would be the signal that the parents have some important work to do on their own and that perhaps they need to be seen alone as a couple for a while. It could also happen that one child is quieter than the others and it is easy to forget he is there. Again, it is necessary to draw out the child rather than assuming that if he is quiet, it must mean that he is fine. If he is quiet in the session, he is probably quiet at home, and this could signify that he is not feeling himself to be a part of the family.

Allowing Scapegoating

Allowing scapegoating to happen in sessions is a huge mistake in family therapy. If everyone is ganging up on one member, it is the therapist's role to try to understand the person who is being scapegoated. If the therapist joins in the scapegoating, she has lost her professional distance and has most likely become too caught up in the family system.

A family with three children and two parents came in together and four of them were actively blaming all the family's problems on the father. The therapist could see the father sinking deeper in his chair, feeling defeated, and simply asked him, "Is this how it is at home?" The father, feeling some compassion from the therapist began to come to life and express his own point of view. It was clear that the family had stopped listening to his side of things a long time ago. As we continued to explore this, it turned out that the mother was regularly disapproving of his behavior in front of the children and they had all lost respect for him. Once the dad got to speak in an authentic way about his feelings of loneliness and isolation from the family, several of the children began to have empathy for him and reached out to him more than they had in a long time.

Mistakes Concerning the Direct Interaction

A number of common mistakes can happen around the direct interaction. As was mentioned earlier in the book, trust must be sufficiently developed before a direct interaction will work. Choosing an angry or resistant member to participate in this two-person encounter is also an error. The idea is to choose people who are "ready" to interact in an honest way so that they can be models for the others to follow. If a direct interaction doesn't work out because the members were not ready to speak in that way, it is unlikely that another one done right afterwards will work out any better. It may be best at that point to let the family talk about what it was like to see these two people having such a hard time trying to talk to each other. Honest conversation about that can allow trust to build up again.

Dean and Molly were the parents in a family of four and came in because of the difficulty their son, Joshua, was having in school. After a check-in, in which it was very clear that mom and dad had a lot of unresolved issues, they were given a chance to have a direct interaction. Dean had said that he was feeling overwhelmed at work and just didn't feel he had much energy left for the family. When the therapist asked Molly how she felt hearing this, she replied, speaking to the therapist, "Oh that's a big lie. He's just making excuses." At that point the therapist realized that, at this moment, Molly was not capable of having empathy for Dean's position or else she was just too angry to access it. To continue in this vein would not have brought Dean and Molly any closer. Instead, the therapist asked the children how they felt witnessing this interaction between their parents. This brought up considerable information about the alliances in the family.

Caretaking as Resistance

One thing that family members often do is protect or caretake each other. This can be another form of resistance for the therapist to be aware of. Amy and her sister, Leslie, came in with their parents, Martin and Jessica. Amy said her problem was that she had a hard time expressing anger in her life and also walked around with a low-level depression much of the time. She was a client in individual therapy, and she thought a family session would be good for her healing because she felt she had learned this behavior in her family. As the session went on, Amy and her mom began having a direct interaction. The therapist was aware that although Amy was telling her mom how angry she was at her, she still wore a big smile on her face the whole time she was saying this. The therapist decided to point this out to Amy, hoping that if Amy became aware of what she was doing, things might change in this interaction. Amy then broke into tears, saying she was afraid to hurt her mom with her anger. It turned out that Jessica, her mom, had a history of depression and that Amy had long ago taken on the role of being mom's caretaker. Had the therapist gotten "caught in the system" and allowed the smile to be there, this dynamic might not have been exposed and a chance for honest conversation between family members might have been missed.

Flight into Health

After a few weeks of doing family therapy, a family may report, "everything is fine." While this could be the truth, it may also be a "flight into health," or an avoidance of going into deeper issues. It would be a mistake for the therapist to: 1) believe everything is fine just because the family said so or 2) not believe everything is fine just because the family said so. Thus, the "everything is fine" is just a starting place for the session. The therapist then needs to probe further with each member of the family and pay particular attention to non-verbal cues in order to find out whether the changes the family had wanted to make have really occurred.

The IP's behavior may have improved considerably, but on further examination it may become apparent that another person in the family is starting to experience difficulty. Or perhaps things have improved somewhat and this is as far as the family wants to go right now. It is important for the therapist to keep an open mind when the family says, "We're fine!"

Closing the Session Too Abruptly

Regardless of one's office situation, it is not a good idea to close the session too abruptly when a member has just experienced strong emotions. The therapist is the timekeeper. She should not begin to facilitate an interaction when she suspects there might not be time to properly conclude it. Especially if one has others waiting to use the office or clients who are in the waiting room, it is important to intervene at five or ten minutes before the time is up and say, "Our time is almost up so let's not begin anything new right now. We want to have time for the check out."

The check-out serves to wrap up the session by including all the members, but also has a grounding effect on the family. For one of the family members to walk out the door in tears can be embarrassing for them and create a sense of chaos in the family.

Discounting the Validity of Individual Therapy and Other Therapies

When one begins to learn the advantages of using a family therapy approach such as CFFT, it can be easy to become a "true believer," and recommend everyone for family therapy. The authors firmly believe that individual therapy, as well as couple and group therapy, can be important healing modalities for clients, depending on their circumstances.

Roberta, a psychology student in training, came from a very dysfunctional family. When she learned of the CFFT approach, she at once wanted to bring her family members into therapy. She had not spoken to them for many years and, when she attempted to open up communication with them, they were not at all receptive. Their motto was "the past is the past," and they were very reluctant to put themselves into a vulnerable situation with the other family members.

Roberta was very disappointed with her family's response but found she could work out many of her issues in longer-term individual psychotherapy with a caring therapist. She also chose to join group therapy where she continued to grow in a group context without her family members. Psychodramatic techniques would have been another option for her had she wanted to work in that fashion.

Thus, the authors are of the belief that healing comes in many forms and that there is no *one* approach that is appropriate for everyone. Working with an individual therapist over a long period of time can allow a client to go to depths he might not be able to reach with his family members present. Group therapy, too, can accomplish many of the benefits that family therapy provides, as group members project many of their family issues on the therapist and other members of the group. What we have found is that the combination of individual therapy and having a few sessions with one's family can be a very powerful combination, especially for adult children.

Summary of Section II

This section looked at the various principles and techniques that are part of Core Focused Family Therapy. The pre-initial session preparation discussed how a therapist should handle an initial phone conversation with a family member inquiring about family therapy, how the therapist chooses to work with a family or not, counter-transference, and who should come to the first session. The check-in section focused on ways to create a safe container for the family to express their core issues. The direct interaction section explored ways that a therapist can set the stage for and use specific interventions to get the most out of a direct interaction between two family members. The check-out section looked at how to close a session, note-taking, subsequent sessions, and termination. Finally, common mistakes frequently made by family therapists were discussed.

Section III

CFFT Modifications

11.
Family Therapy without the Whole Family Present

The final section of this book is devoted to **Psychodramatic Family Therapy** and **Gestalt** techniques that can be used when the whole or part of the family is not able or willing to participate in the family therapy session. These methods can be particularly useful for families with deceased members about whom the members still have unresolved feelings.

Psychodramatic Family Therapy

In a classroom or other group situation such as a Psychodrama Group, **role-playing** can be used as a good substitute for actual family members coming into a session. There are advantages and disadvantages of this method in comparison with an actual family therapy session. One advantage of **Psychodramatic Family Therapy** is that it can be used when family member(s) are deceased, unwilling, or unable to come to sessions. Another advantage is that the **protagonist,** which is what the central figure in psychodrama is called, may say things to the role players who are playing his family members that he would be too cautious to say to his *actual* family members at this point in time. Often, the **psychodramatic** session can be used as a dress rehearsal for the session with the *actual* members present.

For example, Manny's parents were quite old and in poor health when he took the family dynamics class (described later in this section). His father had already had several heart attacks and was in quite a fragile state. However, Manny was still filled with rage about some of the things his dad had done to him in his childhood, which were still affecting his relationships today. Manny felt at this point that he would have to be very gentle with his dad if he actually worked with him in therapy, because if anything happened to his dad as a result of the session, Manny could be living with a lot of guilt for the rest of his life.

In the psychodrama format he was able to unleash some of the rage he felt towards his dad while, later, in his vulnerability, telling him how much he was still suffering from his childhood treatment. The role-player playing Manny's father was very engaged in the role and was able to hear Manny's anger without getting defensive. By the end of the psychodrama, both Manny and the role-player were crying about the pain they had caused each other, and Manny felt much closer to his father. This compassion could then transfer over to his actual dad, even though he was not present in the session.

In a psychology graduate school classroom at the California Institute of Integral Studies in San Francisco, the professor and primary author of this book, Judye Hess, created a technique called **Psychodramatic Family Therapy**. She has been utilizing it with her students, who are therapists in training, for more than 20 years. The class is called Family Dynamics and Therapy and is required for all students in the Integral Counseling Psychology program, a unique, experiential MA program leading to a license in Marriage and Family Therapy. Over the years, the method has been expanded to include having each role player actually call the family member he is role playing in the psychodrama. The role-players are given specific questions to ask the family member, which helps to facilitate their getting to know them in a timely manner. Thus, the role-player gets to have a first-hand sense of the family member whom they are role-playing and can use this information, in combination with the information given to them by the protagonist, when playing the role. Once all the role-players and the protagonist get together to do a family session, the results are very powerful and seem as authentic as if the real family members were actually present in the room. The actual family members are usually very curious to find out how the session went and the conversations between the protagonist and the real members take on a new depth after the psychodramatic family therapy session has taken place. Students often choose to play the audiotape of the session for their families, which brings the family members even more into the process and often motivates the planning of a live family session

The instructions on the class syllabus regarding the **Psychodramatic Family Therapy** sessions are as follows:

Choose a simulated family from the class members to represent your family of origin. Make your selections based on who reminds you of your mother, father, siblings, and other significant people in your life now, or when you were growing up. The person may have similar physical characteristics or just a similar "energy." You may include people who are no longer living, and indeed you should do so if they are in your immediate family. It will be necessary to coach each of the role players as to the personal characteristics of the person they are playing (age, birth order, personality traits, who they were close to or distant from, growing up and presently) as well as current-day facts (geographical location, occupation, marital status, current relationships to all family members) about their lives.

You may also choose to have your role-players actually call up the family member whom they are role-playing in order to get that person's perspective on the family. You (the student) should call the family member in advance to secure permission for this phone call from your classmate. Various forms of phone interviews are possible, from very open-ended to more structured. Ultimately, it is the protagonist who decides whether or not to call the family member and what kind of questioning would be most helpful. You may also have some role players call family members and others not.

Once your role-players have the information needed from you and from the family members, schedule a time before your psychodrama for all the role players to meet. At this meeting, the protagonist can discuss the family rules, coalitions, possible scapegoating, and styles of interaction. The protagonist can also suggest who would sit next to whom, as well as any outstanding non-verbal gestures that each may display. If there are certain styles of dress the members would wear, this can be advised beforehand so the role-player can really "look the part." It is a good idea to bring photos of the original family members in for the role-players to see, and these photos can be shared with the rest of the class after the psychodrama.

The actual psychodrama will be a family therapy session lasting one hour, with myself as therapist and a classmate of your choice as the support person. The support person will sit in with us during the psychodrama, make a few comments at the end, and take the family outside afterwards to de-role the role players.

The de-roling process consists of having all the family members stand in a circle, close their eyes, take a few breaths, and remove the nametag they have been wearing bearing the name of the family member they have been playing. The support person then says to each member in turn, "You are no longer the father; you are (their name)." This ritual allows the role-players to shake off whatever role they have been playing for the last hour and slip back into their own body, so to speak. More recently we have added a somatic component to the de-roling process such that the role-player literally engages in movement to "shake off" that family member.

Protagonists must come in with a presenting problem that is a current problem in their lives today. All the family members and the protagonist are their current ages. The problem should not be directly related to your family of origin, as the purpose of the psychodrama is to connect your presenting problem with your family dynamics. For instance, instead of having the problem be "I can't trust my mother," it should represent a broader life issue such as "I have difficulty trusting women in my life, and I am interested in finding out how this relates to my family dynamics." Consider this assignment as an opportunity to get some help on a real issue that is of concern to you in your life as well as to better understand your family dynamics.

The psychodrama is conducted along the same lines as any other family therapy session described in this CFFT book, with a check-in, direct interactions, and a check out. Following the psychodrama and the de-roling process, the role-players share how they felt about playing their particular role in the family and what insights they may have gleaned from playing this role. Then the other class members who were observing the psychodrama give supportive, heartfelt feedback, sharing how they were affected by the psychodrama. Having this support, as well as being "witnessed" by one's colleagues in a very vulnerable state, creates strong bonding in these classes and is a significant aspect of the healing that takes place. Photographs of the original family members are passed around for students to get a sense of who the "real" family members are.

Since the family members are very aware of the process the protagonist has gone through, it is not unusual for them to call the protagonist after the class to find out how it went. The psychodrama is often a dress rehearsal for having a "real" family session since the family members have become interested in and engaged in the project. At the very least, the students will use the themes and insights that emerged in the Psychodramatic Family Therapy, to take back to their individual therapists for further exploration.

Gestalt Techniques

Another way to proceed with family therapy when a member is not present for the session is by using the **empty chair** technique utilized by Fritz Perls in his Gestalt therapy. The purpose of this technique is to help an individual avoid the intellectualization involved in "talking about" problems and conflicts. (15) Similarly, the use of the empty chair technique in CFFT sessions is to prevent members from "talking about" an absent member, and instead encourages them to speak directly to those members.

Dina, age 34, was very anxious to have her father come to the first family session with her. The two were in the middle of a very long power struggle and, in her opinion, he was punishing her by not coming in. However, her stepmother and her eighteen-year-old half-sister did come in for the session. In the early part of the meeting, Dina spoke of the jealousy she felt towards her sister, Anita, who is the full biological child of these parents and how unloved and estranged she felt from the whole family. Some moving moments occurred between Dina and Anita in which Anita was able to get a much clearer picture of where Dina's animosity towards her had been coming from.

After some significant interactions between Dina and her stepmother Julia, the conversation kept cycling back to the missing father. Following her own sense that "talking about" the father would not lead to much movement, the therapist pulled over an empty chair and suggested that Dina talk to her father as if he were in the chair. When a natural pause came in her "dialogue" with her father, the therapist suggested that Dina switch over to the empty chair and role-play her father speaking back to her. This interaction went back and forth for quite a while with powerful emotions being released by Dina. Finally, when the process slowed down, her stepmother and sister were asked if they had any feelings they wanted to share. The step-mom was struck with how much the conversation sounded exactly like the one Dina had at home with her dad. It was clear that she was feeling much empathy for the pain her stepdaughter was in and was very supportive of her. Anita too shared that she now felt very close to Dina and expressed support in her behalf.

What resulted from the session was a bonding among the three women that had not been able to take place before. The dad was usually present in the family interactions and the step-mom and sister were fearful of dad's anger if they looked like they were siding with Dina in these fights. Dina felt very relieved after the session and felt much less alone now that she had made a connection with her stepmother and sister. As often happens in cases like this, the father consented to come in for the next session.

The empty chair technique is also very useful in families where there is a deceased family member. Putting this person in the empty chair creates the space for any of the family members to say things that they haven't had a chance to say to that person before, thereby allowing them to resolve some of their difficult feelings. Using the empty chair is also helpful in that it provides an opportunity for a family to grieve together for the loss of an important family member if that has not taken place before.

Perls' **empty chair** approach is adapted from Moreno's **role reversal,** a powerful technique used in his psychodrama and considered by many to be the most effective technique in therapeutic role-playing. (16) Moreno made the point that such a procedure is helpful not just for resolving interpersonal issues, but is also helpful in personal self-integration.

In CFFT, the use of the empty chair technique involves the family member reversing roles with herself, or taking turns speaking from each of the two chairs as illustrated in Dina's work above. She is dealing with her internal representation of her father and, by doing so, experiences **intrapsychic** healing and growth. At the same time, she is working on the resolution of an **interpersonal** conflict with her dad, and can benefit from the feedback given her by the other family members.

Summary and Conclusion

This book has described an approach to family therapy called Core Focused Family Therapy (CFFT). Section I discussed the general principles underlying this method, the desirable qualities for practitioners using this approach, and the similarities and differences between this method and other current schools of family therapy. Following this was a description of some general concepts in family therapy, particularly emphasizing the shift from the individual therapy paradigm to the family systems paradigm.

Section II described the nuts and bolts of using CFFT with families. The pre-initial session, the check-in, ten principles for the check-in, the direct interaction, the main principles underlying the direct interaction, the check out, therapist note-taking, subsequent sessions, and termination were all discussed in detail. Following this was a discussion of common mistakes made by family therapists.

Finally, Section III discussed how to use this approach when one or more family members are absent, using **Psychodramatic Family Therapy** and Gestalt "empty chair" techniques.

Judye Hess on the Development of CFFT

I grew up in a family with a dad who was a prominent psychoanalyst in New York City and an older sister who followed in his footsteps to become a psychoanalyst on Long Island. With a background like that, it was pretty clear that I would follow suit in terms of career path. I proceeded to go to graduate school in clinical psychology back in the early 1970s at the University of Rhode Island. While working on my dissertation, I was able to secure a part-time job at a youth guidance center in Worcester, MA. The only problem was, I had never been particularly interested in working individually with children or teens. Lo and behold, I was assigned a supervisor who had been trained at the Ackerman Institute in New York back in the 1960s. Now, mind you, I had never so much as taken a course in family therapy at graduate school since there were no such courses in the curriculum at that time. When Eliot Brown, PhD, my supervisor, saw my reluctance to working individually with the children, he smiled and said, "Well, why don't you see the whole family?" I started to grow pale when he added, "You can tape record the sessions and then I'll go over them with you." That was some relief.

And so began what has been the focus of my personal and clinical odyssey: The Family. Once I found myself sitting in a room with four, five, or even six members of the family, something clicked. I found that this was indeed a natural state for me. I felt at home and seemed to make the family feel at home as well. I realized that I had found a new passion for myself: "work" that I loved as much as any so-called pleasurable activity. I couldn't wait to see the next family! We found a chemistry that allowed for healing to take place in these often multi-problem families. I couldn't have been happier, and so were the families. And so, of course, was my supervisor, who realized he had found a convert to this very new and growing field of family therapy.

I wound up doing my dissertation on adolescent girls and their families and spent that year going to the homes of about fifty families to administer tests to the parents and their adolescent daughters. Meanwhile, I would be sitting and watching TV with the younger children or playing with the family dog or cat. In these often cold winter nights in New England, I found myself as much at home in these family setting as I had felt with families in the therapy room, quite unlike the feelings I had grown up with in my own family. In fact, what was so neat about these situations was that not only were the families being healed...so was I.

Coming out to California in 1977, I was soon to join up with AFTNC (Association of Family Therapists of Northern California), and continue counseling families at the Xanthos Family Counseling Agency (now Alameda Family Services). I remember some of the early AFTNC retreats down at Soquel, CA with Carl Whitaker and Helm Steirlin. I still quote from the conversations that took place with some of those great icons of family therapy.

In 1979 I found a really good mentor to continue my training, none other than past AFTNC president, Alan Leveton, MD. There were only six of us in his yearlong course, Advanced Family Therapy, which met weekly for five hours at the Family Therapy Center on Sacramento Street. We worked on client families, often bringing them to class, as well as our own families of origin. At the time, I was going through a particularly difficult time with my own family. I once brought in a very guilt-inducing letter from my psychoanalyst father to share with the class. I can never forget Alan's almost blasé attitude upon hearing it. He said something like, "Oh, I've seen so many of these letters before.", and was clearly unperturbed. When I conveyed how anxious I was at the idea of seeing my parents coming out to visit me in California, Alan said, "Well, why don't you bring them in? I'll see them with you." WOW! Could this really happen?

I broached the subject with my parents by saying the only way I would be willing to see them was if they agreed to come to family therapy with me. My father, who was very identified with the role of doctor, was not happy with the prospect of being someone else's "patient." But my mom, who had thirty years of unresolved issues to work out with my dad, talked him into it. And so it was...they came out here and we did a six-hour marathon session with Alan, something none of us would ever forget.

In 1984, I was offered a position at the California Institute of Integral Studies teaching Family Dynamics and Therapy. It was my dream of a lifetime and still adds incredible satisfaction to my life. While the nature of the class involved doing psychodramas where students would act out the parts of the family members, as described in this book in "Psychodramatic Family Therapy" on page 124, the last ten years have brought more and more actual families into the classroom for sessions. At times it will be just a parent or a sibling of the student; at other times the student will bring in his or her whole family for the demonstration session. As one student recently remarked in her paper, "When people brought their family members into class, they changed in a moment. They started looking as part of a whole...their faces and their bodies. Everything in them changed. I believe that the reason for that change is the huge potential lying in the family system, a potential for deep intimacy and creativity."

In 1996, I began teaching Family Case Seminar at the Center for Holistic Counseling at John F. Kennedy University in Orinda, CA, and continued teaching there for the next 10 years. Most recently, I have begun teaching Marriage and Family Therapy at Holy Names University in Oakland, CA, and am finding that teaching in an atmosphere of greater diversity has enhanced my learning considerably. I appreciate seeing families and couples who come from very different cultural backgrounds and find this to be a stimulating and rewarding experience for the students and myself.

So when the question comes up, "Are you in this field 'because of' your family?" I cannot deny that growing up in my family has been a significant factor in my career choice. The inherent yearning I have always had to be part of a healing family, my familiarity with deeply embedded dysfunctionality, my skills at being an agent of change, and the inborn passion for this work that I was endowed with in this lifetime have all led to a path that has brought incredible fulfillment to my life.

Footnotes:
1. Sullivan, H.S., *The interpersonal theory of psychiatry.* New York: W. W. Norton, 1953.
2. Buber, Martin, *I and thou.* New York: Charles Scribner's Sons, 1958.
3. Moustakas, Clark, *Existential psychotherapy and the interpretation of dreams.* Northvale, NJ: J. Aronson, 1994.
4. Bugenthal, James, *Psychotherapy and process.* New York: McGraw Hill, 1978.
5. Ackerman, Nathan, *Psychodynamics of family life. New York:* Basic Books, 1958
6. Felder, Richard E., Malone, Thomas P., Warkentin, John, Whitaker, Carl, "Rational and non-rational therapy: A reply.*" Amer. J. of Psychotherapy, Vol. XV,* No. 2, pp. 212-220. April, 1961.
7. Satir, Virginia, *Conjoint family therapy.* Palo Alto, CA: Science and Behavior Books, 1964.
8. Kempler, Walter, *Principles of gestalt family therapy.* Costa Mesa, CA: The Kempler Institute, 1974.
9. Perls, Frederick, *Gestalt therapy verbatim.* Boulder, CO: Real People Press, 1969.
10. Bowen, Murray, *Family therapy in clinical practice.* New York: Aronson, 1978.
11. Minuchin, Salvador, *Families and family therapy.* Cambridge: Harvard University Press, 1974.
12. Minuchin, 1974.
13. Whitaker, C., Napier, A., *The family crucible.* New York: Harper and Row, 1978.
14. Minuchin, 1974.
15. Perls, Frederick, *The gestalt approach and eyewitness to therapy.* Palo Alto, CA: Science and Behavior Books, 1973.
16. Moreno, J.L., Moreno, Z.T., Moreno, J.D. "The discovery of the spontaneous man with special emphasis upon the technique of role reversal." *Group Psychotherapy* 8:103-29, 1955. Reprinted in 1959, *Psychodrama, Vol. 2.* New York: Beacon House pp. 135-58.

Index

abuse, 8
Ackerman, Nathan, 21
Adler, Alfred, 21
alliances, 50
allies, 56, 67
analytical mind, 17
appointments, 43–48
approach, 45
attunement, 15
authentic connection, 75
authenticity, 6, 12, 105
balance, 68
balanced interest, 59
behaviors
    induced, 41
blaming, 7, 77, 89
body language, 87
bonding, 52
boundaries, 15, 24, 49, 110
boundary issues, 47
Bowen, Murray, 19, 21
Bowenian family therapy, 23

broaden perspective, 30
building bridges, 13
caretaking, 6, 114
case notebook, 44
changing the subject, 77
check-in, 49–70, 103, 112
    "here-and-now" questions, 54
    basic information, 52
    finding allies, 56
    first session, 52
    length, 56
    main areas, 52
    motivational questions, 54
    order, 51
    questions, 50
    ten principles, 57
check-out, 101–5, 111, 116
chemical dependency, 40
childhood roles, 6
clarification, 88
clients
    selecting, 43–48

About the Authors

Judye Hess, PhD, received her doctorate in Clinical Psychology from the University of Rhode Island in 1975. She has been on the Core Faculty in the Integral Counseling Psychology program at the California Institute of Integral Studies in San Francisco, since 1984 where she teaches Family Dynamics and Therapy, and Group Dynamics. She has also taught Marriage and Couple Counseling for many years. Judye has taught these classes at many San Francisco Bay Area schools, such as the Institute of Transpersonal Psychology, Saybrook Institute, University of California at Hayward, John F. Kennedy University, Rosebridge Institute, and currently teaches at Holy Names University.

Dr. Hess has a private practice in Berkeley, California, where she specializes in seeing couples and families. Judye has been active in the Northern California Group Psychotherapy Society and the American Group Psychotherapy Association for the last 30 years, and has led numerous groups and workshops for other group therapists on "Interpersonal Gestalt" and Group Process IN THE NOW. She has presented workshops on Psychodramatic Family Therapy at the American Society of Group Psychotherapy and Psychodrama.

Ross Cohen, MA, received his Master's in Counseling Psychology from the California Institute of Integral Studies in 2004. He is a Licensed Professional Counselor with a private practice in Portland, Oregon.